MISSIONARY AND MAORI

'Kiddy-Kiddy . . . A Church Missionary Establishment'
Kerikeri 1819–1860

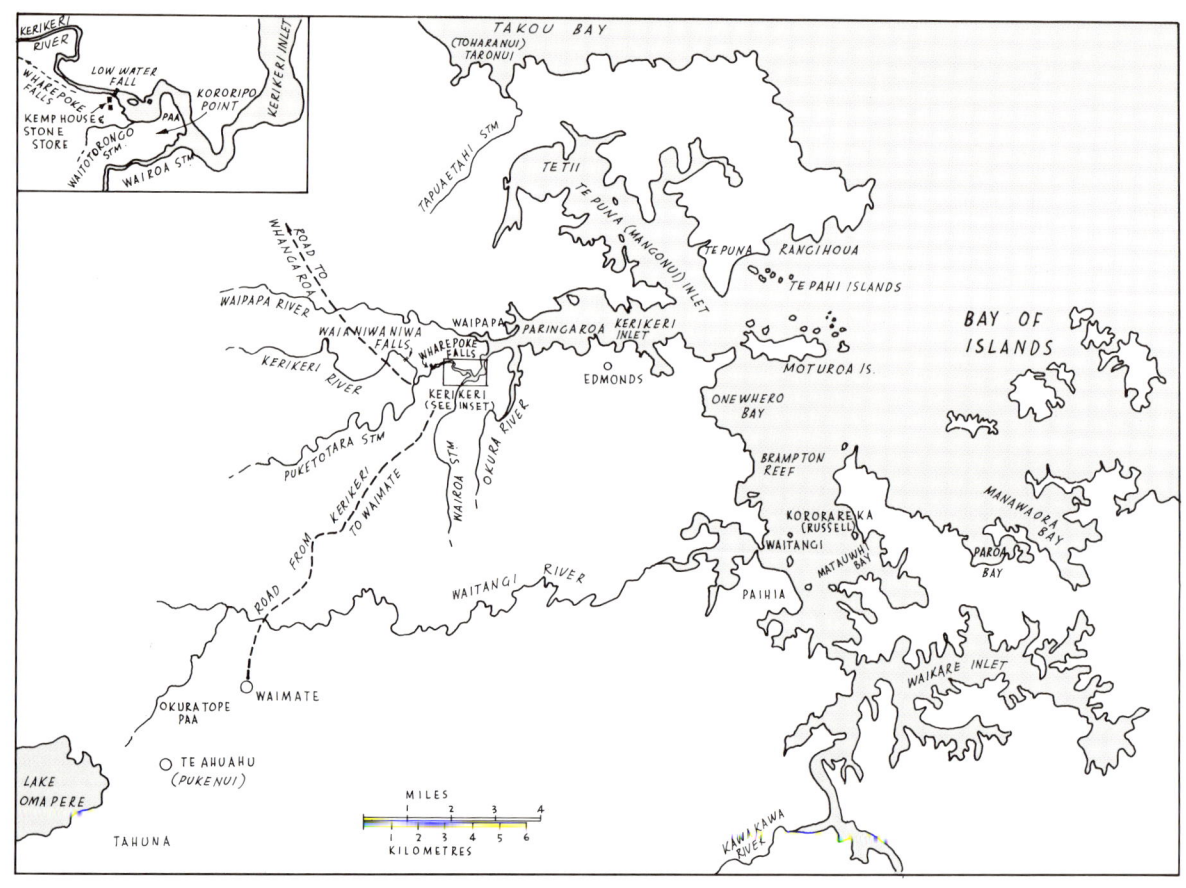

Map of the Bay of Islands showing the settlements and 'roads' in the first half of last century.
FRANK EASDALE

To my husband, Frank

Te Waihora Press,
P. O. Box 57, Lincoln,
New Zealand.

First Published 1991

Copyright © Nola Easdale 1991

All rights reserved

ISBN 0-908714-06-8

No part of this publication may be reproduced, stored in or introduced
into a retrieval system, or transmitted in any form or by any means,
electronic, mechanical, photocopying, recording or otherwise without
the prior permission of the publishers given in writing.

MISSIONARY AND MAORI

'Kiddy-Kiddy . . . A Church Missionary Establishment'
Kerikeri 1819–1860

Nola Easdale

Te Waihora Press

l'étabtissement des Missionnaires an

Kidikidi. — N^{lle} Zélande. —

Cover: *A painting by Augustus Earle entitled 'Kiddy-Kiddy, New Zealand, a Church Missionary Establishment'. The sketch for this painting was probably made by Earle on one of his visits in November 1827. He does not show a striking feature, the bridge over the Waitotorongo Creek which was almost finished at the time he paid a further visit to Kerikeri in April 1828. The boathouse, which he does show, was completed before November 1827. The first chapel (1824) is in the centre of the settlement. The original blacksmith's shop (1819) appears to be still there in front of the store and Hamlin's and Kemp's house. On the hill at the far left is the Maori village. At this time, George Clarke and the Rev. William Yate were living in the Mission House, to the right of which protrudes the large 1822 barn. Across the Kerikeri River is a stable built in 1823. The view is from Kororipo Point. The Maori burial structure appears to be on the point across the river where 'Rewa's Village' is now sited.*
NATIONAL LIBRARY OF AUSTRALIA, CANBERRA

Frontispiece: *The earliest known surviving sketch of the Kerikeri settlement was made in 1824. It is entitled L'etablissement des Missionaires Anglais a Kidikidi Nlle. Zelande. It was the work of a French naval visitor Jules le Jeune. The cluster of buildings on the foreshore include, in front, the blacksmith's shop (1819) (with a privy on the shore). This building did duty as a chapel and wheat store until the first chapel, in the centre of the settlement, was finished in 1824. Behind the old blacksmith's shop are, from left, the storehouse and 'apartments', Kemp's house (1820) and the second smithy. Looking down on the settlement is the Maori village which developed after the arrival of the missionaries.*
MINISTERE DE LA DEFENSE (MARINE), VINCENNES

Contents

Foreword		10
Part I	*The Kerikeri Mission 1819–1860*	
Chapter 1	Whakamaharatanga: A Remembrance	15
Chapter 2	A Highway from the Bay of Islands	21
Chapter 3	Founding the Kerikeri Mission	26
Chapter 4	Troubled Years	35
Chapter 5	Hongi Hika's Return	40
Chapter 6	The New Zealanders' Customs	44
Chapter 7	New Missionaries	54
Chapter 8	Years of Expansion	58
Chapter 9	William Yate's Little Empire	67
Chapter 10	Decline of the Mission	79
Chapter 11	After the Treaty	87
Part II	*The Mission Buildings*	
Section 1	The Mission House	97
Section 2	Chapel, Schoolhouse and Church	117
Section 3	The Stone Store and Mill	126
Section 4	The Wharepoke and Waianiwaniwa Falls	145
Appendix 1	Chronology 1819–1874	151
Appendix 2	Cast	154
Appendix 3	John Gare Butler	156
Appendix 4	Glossary	157
Index		159

Foreword

"The Mission in New Zealand has long been a darling though perhaps a froward child of the parent Society", wrote the Rev. William Yate from Kerikeri in March 1828. The mission station there, after nine years, was in its prime. But its importance was fading in the 1830s and by the 1850s it was no longer one of the Church Missionary Society's stations. Being left to dream in the care of the Kemps was the salvation of its historic buildings.

Of the first three mission settlements in the Bay of Islands, Paihia's buildings have been overwhelmed by later development. At isolated Rangihoua on the Bay of Island's northern shores not a vestige of the houses is left. But Kerikeri has remained relatively untouched over 170 years.

To view the contained Kerikeri Basin from the vantage point of ancient Kororipo Pa, to wander through Kemp House and its garden and into the Stone Store, and in the mind's eye to re-people this small world with the Maori of centuries past and with the first Europeans who made their home here, is to invest that which remains with the spirit of our forebears in a way unparalleled elsewhere in New Zealand.

The Rev. William Williams had written in 1831, 'I trust that our children and grandchildren will behold for years to come, with pleasure and admiration, those exquisite pieces of work which their forefathers accomplished in the infant state of things in this land.' His remarks could apply equally to Maori and Pakeha and to the spiritual inheritance from both.

Kerikeri, as the second Church Missionary Society settlement in New Zealand, was a microcosm of the interaction between the earliest settlers and the tangata whenua. The story, of necessity, is seen through European eyes; it is through the many written records that it is traced. Unfortunately only copied fragments of the journals of two mission wives, Marianne and Jane Williams, are available to us. But the missionary men were charged with writing a daily diary which was sent to England to the parent society. Sometimes there has survived more than one copy of their journals. The contents vary in detail and expression depending on the intended recipient.

In a sense those often ill-educated men were castaways, washed by the evangelical tide that had risen in Europe onto South Pacific shores, where to cling to Christian beliefs and purposes within an utterly strange and strong Maori culture was an exhausting emotional struggle for the mainly youthful brethren. As in the case of the Revs Kendall and Yate, some were broken in the conflict between passions and ideology. Others like James Kemp, although battered by events, were not moved from their rigid beliefs; that they were here to bring the light of Christianity to the darkness of the New Zealander's heathen heart. There is no doubt that in the first years the strength of Maori culture and politics kept the missions in subjection to their protecting tribe and its chiefs. All the missionaries seemed to be doing was clasping their hands in prayer-filled horror as Maori, now armed with muskets, pursued their warlike and cannibalistic customs. It took about fifteen years from 1815 before Christianity made any inroads into the Maori systems of belief. Even then much was accommodated by Maori within their own culture.

Much has been written on the broader aspects of events, politics and the relationships of Maori and Pakeha leading to the Treaty of Waitangi, and its aftermath. This account has a narrower focus — the day-to-day lives of the missionary settlers at Kerikeri and of the tribes who came and went from that place in the years 1819 to about 1860. The basis of this book was originally written as a narrative history of Kerikeri for the Historic Places Trust. A separate text on the Historic Places Trust buildings, Kemp House and the Stone Store, was written for a companion booklet. Eventually the Trust decided to combine the history of Kerikeri and of the historic buildings in one publication.

This decision raised a question: if the story of the buildings was told within a chronological historic sequence, would not the integrity of each building be lost? Further, the flow of the original text would be interrupted while the reader waited for the settlers to put up a frame here, raise a chimney there, shingle a roof or cement some bricks in place. And what would the person who had visited or planned to visit Kerikeri be looking for as he or she flipped through a publication's pages? They would not want details of New Zealand's oldest surviving wood and stone structures buried within the text.

These buildings deserved to stand alone. Consequently the story of the founding of the mission and of the people who lived at Kerikeri is the backdrop against which the buildings rise. The chapter on the chapel/church is included, as the church, now more than a century old, is within the historic precinct of the Kerikeri Basin and a symbol of the purpose which imbued the spirit of the founding evangelists. The section on waterfalls hopes to expand the historic perceptions of those who will walk from the Kerikeri Basin through the Bay of Islands Maritime and Historic Park Board's reserves to view the Wharepoke or Waianiwaniwa Falls.

It will be noticed that 'New Zealanders' is used instead of 'Maori' for the years up to 1828. 'New Zealanders' or 'natives' was used in contemporary writings to refer to the tangata whenua. The first recorded use of the term 'Moudi' was in William Yate's journal of 1828. From then on 'Maori' is used in the text (unless in quotes).

The sources for the text were multitudinous, and in a work of this kind, intended for the general reader, pages of references would have been inappropriate. However, a draft copy of the original historical narrative, together with earlier reports on Kemp House and Stone Store, detail sources of quotations and are held by the Historic Places Trust. As well, working diaries for the years 1819 to 1844 and beyond, compiled from missionary and contemporary accounts, with a card subject index have been deposited at the Auckland Institute and Museum Library.

My grateful thanks are due to all those who helped me to track a path through the jungle of manuscripts and publications — the staffs of Auckland Public Library; Auckland University Library; St John's Theological College Library, Auckland; Anglican Church Archives, Auckland; Department of Survey and Land Information, Auckland; Lands and Deeds Registry, Auckland; National Archives, Wellington; Alexander Turnbull Library, Wellington; Hocken Library, University of Otago; National Library of Australia, Canberra; Dixson Library, State Library of New South Wales, Sydney; Service Historique de la Marine, Ministère de la Défense (Marine), Vincennes; and most particularly the staff of the Auckland Institute and Museum Library. And to the people who shared their knowledge and gave support — Jack Lee, Peter O'Hagan, John Stacpoole, John Webster, Verna Mossong and the late Ruth Ross; staff of the Historic Places Trust, Patricia Adams, John Wilson and Margaret Long; Sydia and the late Rangi Marsh of Te Ahuahu; Annette Singh; Rie Fletcher; and my friend Noni Kenny who cheerfully and patiently typed several manuscript drafts — thank you all.

One thing remains to be said. Should Kerikeri rightfully be Kirikiri? It would seem so. The meaning of 'Kirikiri' is gravel, a name applied by Maori to many New Zealand rivers. At Kerikeri it was the name of the river which flowed into the basin, but this was extended in missionary times to the tidal inlet by which Kerikeri was reached. In 1827 (when the orthography of a written Maori language was being settled) 'Kiddeekiddee' (or similar phonetic spelling) became Kerekere. Even then William Yate wrote in June 1829 'Te Kerikeri, pronounced Kedeekedee meaning gravel . . .' Other writers also gave the meaning as gravel. 'Keri' means to dig. It is clear that the later meaning 'dig dig' was given to the word after the spelling Kerikeri had become fixed.

N.B. This foreword was written in January 1988 at the request of the

Historic Places Trust which had long since accepted and already edited the manuscript for publication. By March 1988 circumstances had changed and word was received that the Trust would, regrettably, be unable to proceed with publication. Little has been altered in the book now offered from that which the Trust had intended to publish. I am especially indebted to John Wilson, of Te Waihora Press, editor of *New Zealand Historic Places*, for his consistent support and friendship over many years.

Nola Easdale.
February 1989.

Hongi Hika and Waikato, drawn in London at the time of their visit with Kendall in 1820.
HOCKEN LIBRARY, DUNEDIN

Chapter 1

Whakamaharatanga: A Remembrance

'Although I die there is an aute tree that has been planted by me beside the wall of my house.' The ariki, about to be slain in battle, flung this challenge at his foe. His dignity as a chief was hereditary. He was the Take o te Whenua — the root of the land — his being in and with the land. The land was Aotearoa and his tribal place; his hereditary mana derived from the long line of ancestors stretching back to the traditional homeland Hawaiiki where the aute had flourished. His tree — this seed — would be strong to avenge his death. His mana was with his successor and with the tribe.

The custom of planting a piece from a tree at the birth of a child was recorded in the Bay of Islands at the time of early European contact. A stick was broken in half and the navel cord and placenta buried with the planted stick. The other portion was given to a relative who 'gnawed upon it' then cast it away to dissolve the charm. Afterwards the infant could be brought into the camp of his people. If the planted stick grew strongly, so should the child.

Centuries ago the tangata whenua had come from Eastern Polynesia bringing with them the traditions of a homeland, Hawaiiki. In the north of New Zealand the climate favoured the growth of the taro, the kumara, the hue, and the aute, which had come with them. The people flourished, and divided into many hapu. The pressure on the land and its bounty became great. Quarrels arose between the hapu, battles were fought and some of the people set out to find other places to live. Their canoes carried them to many parts around the coast of New Zealand. Traditions tell of their sometimes finding other people at these places with whom they joined; at others the land was open for them to settle.

An old manuscript of Ngapuhi origin tells of early migrations from the north. The famous canoes

> *Te Arawa, Takitimu, Kurahaupo, Nainaimoko, Hourata, Tainui . . . came from here. They were built by the men of Whangaroa on the farther side of Tokerau (Northland). Some belong to Takou, above Te Puna. All the canoes of Rahiri and others belonged to there. Some of the canoes belonged to Waipapa, in the fresh water of Kerikeri. Some came from Rangiawa River below Whangaroa. Many were the villages where the canoes were built. I heard from my elders that all the canoes came from there.*

Over the generations there were a number of migrations from what may have been 'the last Hawaiiki, Muriwhenua', the north. Traditional accounts, waiata and genealogies link the tribes of Northland to the East Coast, from Coromandel to Whakatane to Hawke's Bay, and tell also of journeys back from the East Coast to the North.

It was to Kerikeri that the great chief Kauea came in times past — who knows when? — 'from Whakatane on a war of invasion through Waikato, Tamaki, and the Kaipara, extending his warfare to the far north'. He made peace with those districts and his son Toko O Te Rangi settled at Kaipara marrying a Kaipara chieftainess of the Ngati Awa tribe. In time Kauea emerged in whakapapa as a semi-deified ancestor of Ngapuhi. His name was one in the long line of ancestors recited during the sacred rites for the lifting of tapu. Kauea became symbolised in tales as a taniwha, 'who went underground and came out above at Kerikeri'.

Once, the powerful Ngati Awa tribe had dominated the north from Whangarei to Cape Reinga.

> *When the Ngapuhi area was occupied by Ngati Kahu (a 'second name' for Ngati Awa) all the good places were cultivated and their food pits are open to this day on the tops of hills everywhere in the area. The burial places are kept sacred by Ngapuhi and their bones are dust . . .*

The northern tribal name of Ngapuhi is said by some to be derived from Puhi-moana-ariki who returned from Whakatane. Like his forebear Kauea he was also of the line of tapu removers. But 'real men' began with Puhi Moana Ariki's son (or grandson) Rahiri, their descendant. Rahiri lived in the seventeenth century and is the ancestor of the present Ngapuhi, Rarawa and Aupouri tribes of Northland. It was from Rahiri's time that Ngapuhi, then confined to the Hokianga area, began the process of penetration from the western to the eastern coast. Although most Ngati Awa had long gone southward, a few tribal remnants remained. About Waimate, inland from Kerikeri, a Ngati Awa hapu, Ngati Miru, were settled. Driven from this desirable place by the emergent

An ink drawing of 'Native Chiefs' by W. Bambridge. The chiefs are, left to right, 'Hakiro', 'Nene Waka' and 'Rewa'. The original is in the W.C. Cotton Journal.
DIXSON LIBRARY, SYDNEY

Hokianga Ngapuhi they fled to the Kerikeri and Mangonui Inlets. In about the middle of the eighteenth century the chief Auha (grandfather of Hongi Hika who would later befriend the missionary settlers) and his half-brother Whakaaria leading a Ngapuhi force, took Kerikeri from the Ngati Miru, who scattered, fleeing to Whangaroa.

Kororipo Point and the Wairoa Stream at Kerikeri became from this time the seaport of Ngapuhi. An old name for the pa on the point, or the waters of the inlet leading to it, may have been Te Waha o Te Riri — The Mouth of Anger, or The Inlet of War. The jawbone of Mahiapoake, great-grandson of Rahiri, and great-grandfather of Auha, was said to lie buried on the banks of the inlet near to this place. The waka taua which were made ready at the Kerikeri, were exercised before departure on this stretch of water, gathering to them the mana of this ancestor. Guarding the head of the inlet, near to the mission settlement, the pa (now known as Kororipo Pa) may be an old one, originally that of the Ngati Awa tribe. In the time of Auha and his son Te Hotete it was likely to have been fortified, the canoes drawn to safety within the palisading. When the missionaries came to Kerikeri, Hongi Hika's main pa Okuratope was at Waimate, and Kororipo Pa appears to have been disused as a fortification.

'Pancho to the life'. The ariki Tareha, drawn by W. Bambridge in 1844. The picture comes from the W. Cotton Journal
DIXSON LIBRARY, SYDNEY

Auha's son Te Hotete had set out from this seaport to descend more than once on the Ngaere Raumati tribes on the southern side of the Bay of Islands. Vengeance was sought for the earlier slaying of Te Hotete's wife and daughter at Waimate. (These women were the mother and sister of Hongi Hika's half-brothers, chiefs Rewa and Moka, who would also play an important part in the lives of the missionaries at Kerikeri.)

A famous sea battle took place off Tapeka Point (near Russell). An important Ngaere Raumati chief was killed and the triumphant Ngapuhi returned to Kerikeri with his head, where it was set upon a rock by the water, not far from Kororipo Point. This rock is known as Te Karu o Te Tawheta — the Head of Te Tawheta.

The Ngati Rehia tribe who had, following the rout of Ngati Miru, occupied all the land from Waimate through to Kerikeri and from the Mangonui Inlet to Takou, were not a tribe which could be swept away as Ngati Miru had been and with this tribe Ngapuhi Hokianga had intermarried. The giant chief Tareha and his brother Pakira were both Ngati Rehia, and allies of Hongi Hika, who himself had connections through his maternal grandfather with the coastal people of Te Puna, where he had land in mission times. Tareha had land interests in the Waimate area.

The history of the inland and coastal tribes, and of Tareha, Hongi Hika, Rewa, Moka and others, became increasingly woven into the story of the traders, whalers and missionary settlers who came to the Bay of

Islands in the nineteenth century. Armed with muskets, the profits of trade with the shipping, the tribes joined forces to war against the southern tribes. Hongi Hika rose to prominence as a warrior leader. In the end, he was to die from being wounded by a musket ball; the guns which he had so avidly sought, the cause of his passing. His remains were eventually taken inland through Kerikeri, to lie with his tupuna.

A pihe was composed for Hongi Hika by Turi Katuku expressive of the sorrow of the people at the passing of the age of the great warriors.

Maori	English
E pakukau ana ngai wai o Wharepoke	Slap, slap, murmur the waters of Wharepoke
Ninihi Kau ana nga tai o Kerikeri.	Stealthily flow the tides of Kerikeri.
Tera pea koe ka tuku atu ana	'Twas there, perhaps, that you released
Nga waka hoehoe ki runga o to Kaipuke	The paddling canoes of the great ship.
Kaupapa a waka i roto Waipara	A fleet of canoes floating within Waipara
Me ko Tama-a-rahi, nana i here mai.	And Tama-a-rahi, 'twas he who tied them fast.
Kawa taua ra te kawa i a 'Pango	Only we two remain of the line of 'Pango
Ka hari ra e te wahine 'Ati Manu	By the woman of 'Ati Manu to be carried on and lost with her
Ka riro i a ia.	(A burning mountain)(stands)(within Pupuke)
Na	
Ka ngaro ra e, ko te to whare o te riri	Gone now, is the house of war,
Kei hea hoki ra to pu tangi ata	Where is thy trumpet which was wont to sound at early dawn?
E tau te wheoro he moana pouri	Comes now the rumbling sound, a dark and gloomy sea.
Tuhia karewa te toto aku hoa	With floating drifting streamers
Tuhia ana i te rangi	The blood of these my friends
Ee	Is written in the sky.

By the time this lament was chanted, the mission flag Rongo Pai had been raised in many places, proclaiming the good news that peace reigned there. But this would be many years after the planting of the first Church Missionary settlement at Rangihoua in December 1814.

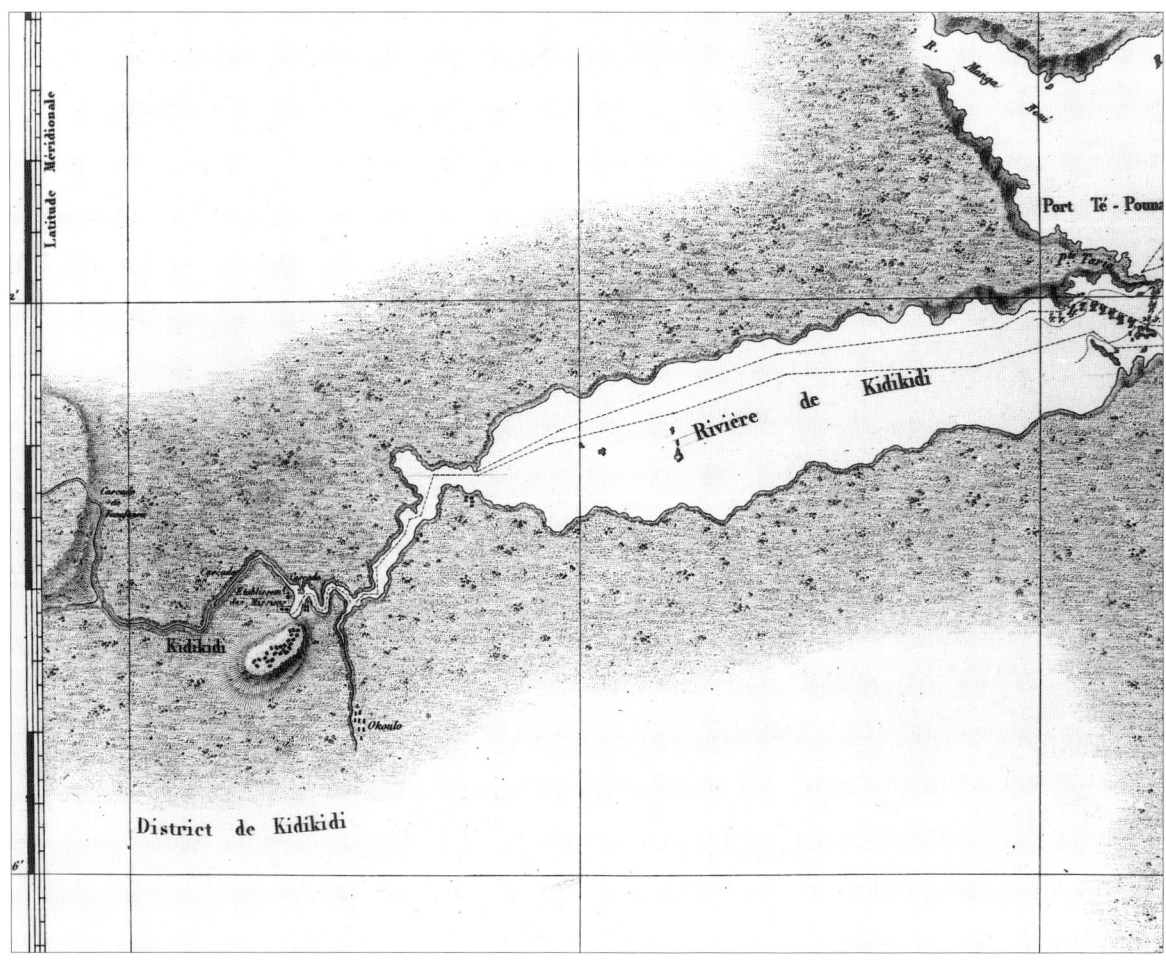

A map of the Kerikeri Inlet from the French Atlas Hydrographie. *The map was compiled from the Duperrey survey of 1824 and some later work by Dumont d'Urville, 1826-27.*
AUCKLAND INSTITUTE AND MUSEUM

Chapter 2

A Highway from the Bay of Islands

In the 'vast, safe bay of Tippouna' sheltering behind Moturoa Island, near the mouth of the Kerikeri Inlet lay, in March 1810, four whalers and a sealer, put in at the Bay of Islands for supplies from the New Zealanders. The news of the burning of the ship *Boyd* in Whangaroa Harbour, and the massacre of nearly all aboard had reached them. Having, as they later wrote, every reason to believe that the chief Te Pahi of Te Puna had been responsible for this massacre the men from the ships set out one night in the ships' boats for Te Pahi's island, to rescue, they said, any so fortunate as to escape and to 'recover the arms, ammunition, and other warlike stores from the hands of the savages'. Landing on the island and advancing to the village, the contingent found 'the natives in a hostile disposition' and soon had a volley of musketry and spears discharged at them. The island was taken by force of arms and Te Pahi, wounded, fled the place with other survivors.

Other contemporary writers expressed horror at what they saw as the indiscriminate slaughter of the guiltless inhabitants, the burning of the whare (including a prefabricated house — a gift to Te Pahi by the Governor of New South Wales) and the destruction of the plantations. None more so than the Rev. Samuel Marsden, who as the agent for the Church Missionary Society was hoping soon to establish a mission station in New Zealand under the protection of Te Pahi with whom he had had close contact during Te Pahi's visit to New South Wales. He, and others, contended that even though Te Pahi had been in Whangaroa at the time of the sinking of the *Boyd*, he had been a helpless bystander, and that his name had been confused with that of Te Puhi, a chief of Whangaroa. Whatever the truth, this terrible sequence of events was to set back the founding of the New Zealand mission for almost four years.

The whalers who had exacted this ruthless revenge on Te Pahi were still at anchor when William Leith arrived at the Bay of Islands in April. Leith had been sent by a merchant company in New South Wales to investigate the setting up of a flax works in New Zealand and to examine other productions of the country. With most of the warriors away from the Bay on a war expedition, Leith and his companions felt it safe to go exploring. 'After reaching the head of the river' Leith later reported to the merchant house, 'we landed and penetrated about ten miles inland'. It would appear from other hints in his letter that this 'river' was the Kerikeri Inlet. Though short on description, it is the first recorded European account of a penetration inland from the Kerikeri waterway.

The Rev. Samuel Marsden and his friend John Nicholas had little more to say of the Inlet when they came up it to the Kerikeri Basin in 1815 and went on to Lake Omapere. On his second visit to the Bay in 1819, Marsden was forced by the ebbing tide to go ashore and remarked on a very large cockle bed, dry at low water where about a hundred women were busy collecting cockles for food. Nearby was a village. The cockle beds belonged strictly to certain tribes. Their extent and ownership were marked by poles, sometimes with old flax mats hung upon them. Violation could bring retribution (or be used as an excuse for such) when, as was the case in 1819, Hongi's slaves gathered cockles from a bed in the Kerikeri Inlet, tapu to his enemy Te Morenga and his tribe. Twenty of Hongi's war canoes were subsequently burnt at Kerikeri and a fight took place inland near Taiamai.

The Rev. Henry Williams, arriving in August 1823, was 'struck with the appearance of vast numbers of wild duck . . . which had been reported in this quarter — but upon drawing nearer, we discovered that it was a considerable quantity of children in the water collecting cockles.'

Fragments of other journals add to the picture of the waterway which ran to the Kerikeri Basin. Richard Cruise in 1820 saw here 'a great number of wild ducks and curlews; some of which were shot and proved very good.' The Duperrey expedition of 1824 noted that 'On the swampy margins some scattered huts can be seen.' Samuel Stutchbury (a zoologist who incidentally gave his name to the New Zealand cockle — *chione stutchbury*) remarked in 1826 on beaches of 'Fine white shell sand consisting wholly of broken cockles'. The Colonial Botanist of New South Wales, Alan Cunningham, left perhaps the best description of the inlet as it was in 1826. Entering the waterway he wrote:

> *we had to contend with a violent north wind and a tide at the last qr of the Ebb against us. About 5 miles from the Entrance we had the young flood in our favour, & occasionally a wind to fill our sail, whilst we were passing the*

> *narrows bounded by mudflats covered with a Cockle (Cardium) which the natives & more especially those often females were gathering together in baskets for food. It was with no small joy these poor Women received from us . . . a few fish-hooks in Exchange for several Baskets of their shellfish, which in the Evening presented our Native boatmen an ample satisfying repast. From that undulation of surface, so characteristic of the shores of the Bay the land progressively flattens, so as to Admit of the Tillage and general Cultvn of the Soil much more easily, than at any stations in the Bay, still however naturaly [sic] clothed with a density of Brake . . . without Trees the latter being remarked in the hollows or small Ravines.*

The areas of tillage would be the patches of potato plantations amongst the bracken covered hillsides, the produce of which the tribes bartered with either the ships in the Bay, or with those which came up the inlet to the end of the deep water, about opposite Parengaroa, now called Skudders Beach.

The artist traveller Augustus Earle, in November 1827, reaching the inlet after dark with his party

> *observed a light from the shore and made for it; but it being low water our boat stuck fast in the slime long before we reached the banks; we were, consequently, obliged to wade knee-deep through the slippery mud. We soon discovered a party of women sitting round a fire made in the midst of the swamp. They had come here for the purpose of procuring shellfish; and as they are never fastidious about shelter or dry beds, they had determined . . . to pass the night where they had been occupied during the day . . . The moment we were seated the water began to ooze an inch or two all round us. We sought in vain for a dry place, for we were enveloped in darkness, and surrounded by rushes and flags six or seven feet high . . . we slept, notwithstanding the misery of a wet bed, with a cloud of fog for curtains. I did not wake until one of the women gave me a good shake . . . They had prepared us a breakfast of hot shellfish . . . we had some biscuits in our boat . . . and gave our "fair founders of the feast" a share; and we were all very sociable and merry. When we left them, as it was again low water, the women carried us to our boat, and took their leave of us amidst peals of laughter.*

A vivid memory of the Rev. Richard Taylor on his arrival in 1839 was the sight of an island covered in the native red kaka beak shrub — the Kowhai Ngutu Kaka of the Maori. Taylor recorded a tale told him by a Maori that the profusion had resulted from a box of seed spilled there, plunder from the ill-fated du Fresne expedition of 1772. He had never found the shrub, he added, except where pa or cultivation had existed. 'The natives greatly admire its rich flowers as an ornament for the ear . . .'

The first missionary settlers at Kerikeri in 1819, even if they had observed all these features of the inlet, wrote little about them. Their journals carry accounts of backstraining efforts to tow rafts of timber or row quantities of stores up the waterway to the infant settlement. Samuel Marsden had, with his friend John Nicholas, come up to the Kerikeri in January 1815. 'The spot where we landed was a small plantation of potatoes belonging to Shunghi [Hongi], and here our party intended to prepare their refreshment'. An umu was dug and fires made within. The fire was raked out, the nicely scraped potatoes bedded in wet grass were laid on the hot stones and covered with earth. While the potatoes steamed, Marsden, hearing the sound of a very heavy fall of water, went to investigate. Climbing the Kororipo ridge, dividing the Wairoa Creek from the Kerikeri Basin, Marsden saw the Kerikeri River falling nine feet into the placid Basin. Here, he wrote, was a natural dam, which could turn a water mill for a new settlement without the expense and risk of making a dam. Here indeed was the ideal place for the second mission station to be planted under the protection of Hongi Hika.

Four years later, in May 1819, John King, Thomas Hansen and the Rev. Samuel Leigh (the latter prospecting in New Zealand for a site for a Wesleyan Station) came through Kerikeri from Rangihoua on their way to the Hokianga Harbour.

Mr Hansen and I accompanied the Rev. W. Leigh to the Kiddee Kiddee . . . where was a Chief left in charge of a few captives to cultivate the land . . . We took a review of their Farms, and judged that between 20 and 30 acres were in cultivation, and they are clearing more. This is pleasing and promising.

This plantation was likely to have been on the gentle sunny slopes on the south side of the Wairoa Stream. The seed wheat which Kendall and King sowed at Kerikeri in August 1819 may have been in this newly cleared ground. The second contingent of missionaries also arrived in August 1819 and it was to the Kerikeri they were to go, where till this time the scrub had covered the ground where they would build the first houses and sow the first seeds.

Another four years on, in August 1823, Marianne Williams, newly arrived in New Zealand, saw a different scene, as she rounded Kororipo Point into the Kerikeri Basin:

we had a delightful row up to Kiddeekiddee. The river wound like a corkscrew; and the banks were in some places very pretty, fringed with low shrubs. The native huts we beheld with curiousity on the top of rocks, and Shunghee's rude palace. The men, who rowed the boat, were fine, intelligent, active-looking lads talking with great animation to Mr Turner . . . On a sudden and

complete turn of the river Kiddeekiddee opened upon us, quite in appearance a little lake with a pleasing fall of water. The situation was beautiful, but wanted wood. The native settlement was upon the hill or rather ridge of hills, and upon the beach the refreshing sight of Mr Butler's and Mr Kemp's English-looking houses. The flag was up, and a musket fired twice in honour of our arrival.

This was Kerikeri a short four years after Marsden had chosen the basin as the site of the second mission station. But it was the Rev. Samuel Marsden's first visit in December 1814 which had laid the foundations of the Church Missionary Society in New Zealand.

William Hall wrote of a scene such as this in May 1819, when he described 'Kiddee Kiddee' as 'a settlement belonging to Shunghee, where was a Chief left in charge of a few captives to cultivate the land'. The picture comes from Dumont d'Urville's Voyage Pittoresque Autour du Monde.
AUCKLAND INSTITUTE AND MUSEUM

Chapter 3

Founding the Kerikeri Mission
1819–1820

'Consider the honour that is put upon you; you are gone to prepare the way of the Lord, to make ready a people for Him.' wrote the Rev. Samuel Marsden to the New Zealand settlers in February 1819. In December 1814 the first Church Missionary Society station in New Zealand had been settled on the northern shore of the Bay of Islands at Rangihoua. Here, five years on, the mission buildings crouched behind high paling fences close by the pebbly beach at the toe of the dominating Rangihoua Pa. Exposed to cold winds, the steep slopes had yielded little produce from the efforts of cultivation by these first missionaries.

To 'make ready a people' the missionaries had been meant to show by example and instruction the advantages of civilisation. The New Zealanders would see how comfortable European cottages were, how efficient the iron tools, how useful domestic animals might be, to appreciate the 'decency' of being 'properly clothed', and what it meant to enjoy the fruits of agriculture — a 'wheaten loaf'. While teaching these skills the missionaries would acquire the key to their success, the New Zealand language. The New Zealanders would become carpenters, blacksmiths, weavers, ploughmen and farmers. For Samuel Marsden it would be 'a joy inexpressible to see the New Zealander returning home from his cultivated field with his sheaf with him'. With the gathering of the wheat sheafs the soul of the New Zealander would also be harvested for the Lord. Tribal wars would be given up, the peaceful arts pursued, and the missionary now skilled in the language, would open their eyes to the sinfulness of man. In recognising this their hearts would be ready to receive the word of God and finally when life closed, their soul would be gathered by their Redeemer into life everlasting.

It hadn't worked out that way. The wheat crop was poor; no souls had

The Church Missionary settlement of Rangihoua, on the northern side of the Bay of Islands, with Rangihoua Pa on the hill to the left. Thomas Kendall, William Hall, John King and their families founded the mission in 1814. This depiction of Rangihoua was published in the **Missionary Register** *in 1832.*
AUCKLAND INSTITUTE AND MUSEUM

been harvested. The missionaries, for their survival, were forced to barter for muskets and powder through the whaling and sealing ships which came to 'water and wood' in the Bay of Islands. Bitterness and quarrels arose among the families in their isolation.

Now, in August 1819, Samuel Marsden had returned to New Zealand to establish another mission station at Kerikeri. Under the protection of the important chief Hongi Hika (who had been to Sydney in 1814), in a place with a kindlier aspect than Rangihoua, well watered, away from the shipping, with more fruitful land backed by extending plains, and on the traditional way to the sea of the numerous inland tribes, this station would surely succeed. Marsden secured from Hongi Hika and Rewa approximately 13,000 acres around Kerikeri for the Church of England Missionary Society and optimistically wrote, 'I thought this land would answer well for any poor labouring Families at any future period should any come out under the Patronage of the Society or their Friends.'

With Marsden there had come as missionaries for the Kerikeri Station the Rev. John Butler, his wife (whose first name is unknown), daughter Hannah (Anne) (aged two), their son Samuel Butler (aged nineteen), Francis Hall (school teacher), James Kemp (blacksmith) and wife Charlotte. As 'mechanics' employed by the mission were William Puckey (carpenter and former ship's commander) who had been with the London Missionary Society to Tahiti from 1796 to 1798, his wife, son William (aged fourteen) and younger daughter Elizabeth, William Fairburn (carpenter) and his wife, and William Bean (carpenter), his wife and infant son. The families stayed with the Kendalls, Halls and Kings at the Rangihoua Station for the next few months.

The Rev. John Butler was New Zealand's first clergyman. He had offered his services as a missionary in 1817, together with those of his son Samuel, and was ordained Deacon in June 1818 at Wells. Butler was ordained Priest on 15 November 1818 by the Bishop of Gloucester and although originally destined for Sierra Leone, sailed from London with his family for New South Wales on 15 December 1818. The settlement at Kerikeri was named Gloucestertown by Butler after his ordinating bishop, a grand name which survived no longer than the first flush of evangelical enthusiasm. Each of the mission families was to have a house and garden, the property of the mission. The mission trade and supplies were to be held in a common store and distributed according to need, and rations were to be issued to each family.

But first the houses had to be built. During August and September 1819 ground near the Waitotorongo Creek was cleared of scrub, the mission buildings laid out, and a temporary raupo hut built to house the carpenters, Bean and Fairburn. In ten days they had the first building up, the blacksmith's shop, twenty-one feet by fifteen feet. This was home for a few months for the carpenters, and a roof for the other men of the mission who, still living with their families at Rangihoua, toiled to tow rafts of logs up the Kerikeri Inlet from the timber grounds some twenty miles away at Waikare and Kawakawa. The second building was a small wooden house, thirty feet by seven feet for the natives to sleep in — the New Zealanders who, exchanging their labour for axes, iron and hoes, worked at the sawpits, back from the present wharf. The third building was the mission store, sixty feet long by fifteen feet wide.

Five days before Christmas 1819, the mission families and their goods were loaded on the punt at Rangihoua and were towed by two large canoes manned by one hundred New Zealanders up to Kerikeri. Into the partitioned store, unlined and with an earthen floor, and probably raupo thatched, went the Butlers and their servant Richard Russell, the Fairburns, the Puckeys and the Beans, the latter now with an extra infant born at Rangihoua. And into the also incomplete blacksmith's shop went the Kemps and Francis Hall.

Outhouse kitchens were built at the rear with chimneys of bricks made by George, a New Zealander who had learnt this art in New South Wales. Around the structures a split pale fence was put up 'to keep the natives from ye doors'. About an acre of land had been broken up and grape vines, Indian corn, a great variety of garden seed and fruit trees (stones,

Founding the Mission

pips, nuts) had been planted. Cattle brought up by punt were turned loose to forage on the native grasses.

The quarters of the missionaries were primitive. Ensign McCrae who visited the infant settlement in March 1820 wrote:

> *The houses are similar to those at Ranghe-hoo having high barricades and wicket doors and like those are far from being clean or comfortable in fact not so much so as those of the natives who tho' not boasting the advantages of civilisation are superior to the missionaries in these respects.*

With the advent of the mission a large, straggling village of native whare had grown up on the ridge behind and overlooking the mission buildings. To the south it sprawled down towards the Wairoa Stream, the seaport of the Waimate tribes. The chiefs Hongi Hika, Rewa, Tareha, Titore, Tinana and Wharerahi stayed in this village when down from the pa around inland Waimate, on their way to fight, to take pigs and potatoes by canoe to trade for muskets and powder with the ships in the Bay, or to meet with sailors in the ships' boats which now began to come up to Kerikeri to trade. When Ensign McCrae's party came up one night to the mission in 1820, their passage around the winding waterway was guided by the light of fires which the natives had made on the banks of the river. William Jowett, accompanying him, recorded

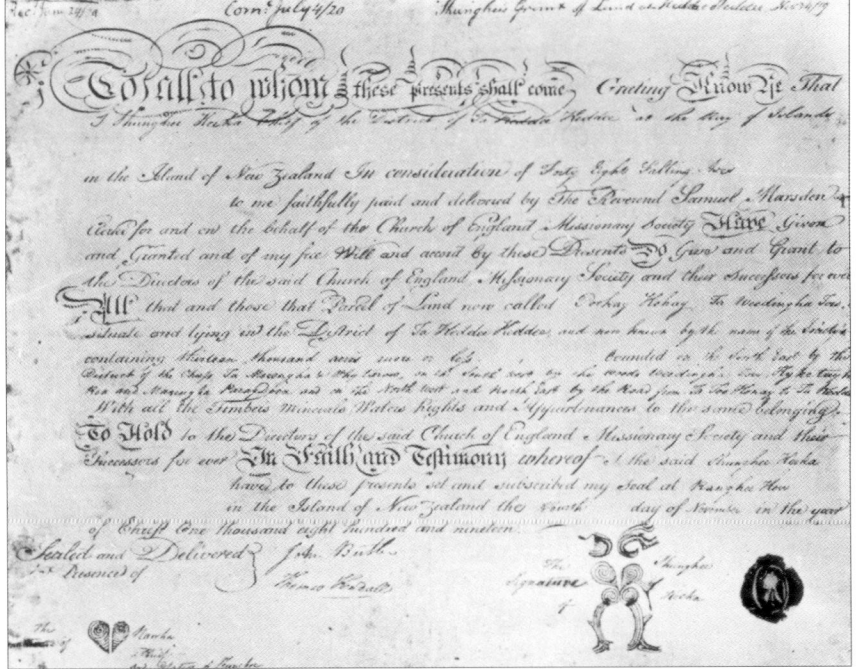

Facsimile of a deed dated 4 November 1819, signed by the Rev. John Butler, Thomas Kendall, with the moko as signatures of Hongi Hika and Rewa.
HOCKEN LIBRARY, DUNEDIN

A trading schooner surrounded by the canoes of New Zealanders. The scene comes from Dumont d'Urville's Voyage Pittoresque Autour du Monde.
AUCKLAND INSTITUTE AND MUSEUM

> . . . *there was a Grate Number of the Natives about the settlement and they Had a Number of Mens Heads to Exchange for Axes or Powder and it was a Wet Wind.*

Both Ensign McCrae and William Jowett had come on the government storeship *Dromedary* which was to seek a cargo of timber in New Zealand. Marsden, also aboard, making his third visit, was to act as an intermediary between the crews of the government ships and the New Zealanders. As a result he hoped for a permanent intercourse between the British Government and New Zealand. The Commanders of His Majesty's ships would recommend on their return to England the formation of a small settlement in the Northern Island. Its 'regular government', it was thought, would be an advantage to the New Zealander. Marsden for a time thought that Hongi Hika might become 'King of the New Zealanders in the North', but the autonomy of the chiefs and intertribal jealousies made this idea impossible. Hongi Hika, knowing his countrymen, opposed this proposal.

Marsden had brought over from Australia three horses for Kerikeri, and sixteen head of cattle and sundry stores for the New Zealand mission.

Bullocks had also been brought to drag spars from the bush. A team of six bullocks was lent to the missionaries. A plough was already in the store, and on 3 May 1820 it was, wrote the ecstatic John Butler,

> *for the first time put into the land of New Zealand at Kiddeekiddee . . . I trust this day will be remembered with gratitude, and its anniversary kept by ages yet unborn. Each heart rejoiced in this auspicious day, and said "May God speed the plough".*

The tangled strength of the bracken roots resisted even the power of the bullocks and the six acres was ploughed twice, but two weeks later the sown wheat was springing up. But there were no fences and this promising crop was chewed down and had to be resown; for farm they must if they were not to starve — or so Marsden said.

James Shepherd, 'a pious young man', born in New South Wales had also come with Marsden to join the mission at Kerikeri. He was to live during the week some miles away from the station in a little hut at Okura, up a branch of the Kerikeri Inlet, planting a nursery of crops and fruit trees to distribute amongst tribal chiefs. Shepherd was to have a difficult time at Okura. Marsden had placed him there to appease the chiefs Te Morenga and Perahiko, enemies of their neighbours inland — the Waimate/Kerikeri tribes who would benefit from the settlement at Kerikeri. Shepherd's mana was low in the New Zealanders' eyes, being regarded as a 'slave' sent by Marsden to Okura as utu for the death of Perahiko's son in Sydney. His situation was made more difficult by the Okura people's refusal to barter with him. Marsden had set aside a sum of £30 for expenses at Okura. Butler, jealous of Shepherd's independence and wanting him back at Kerikeri, made many gifts of goods to the Okura tribe. Now they expected the same favours from Shepherd. Unable to barter, he was almost starved out, but persevered, planting peas, beans, turnips, wheat (which a flood washed away) and fruit tree stones, until October 1820 when he returned to New South Wales to seek a wife.

The scorn of the tribes was not directed at Shepherd alone. The New Zealanders at Kerikeri looking down upon the mission from their hillside village despised those labouring to build and plant, saying they would be no more than 'cookees' in their own country, England. The mechanic, however, was held in esteem for his skills, particularly those which the New Zealander could make use of. James Kemp the blacksmith who had built his forge early in 1820 had been directed by the Church Missionary Society

> *on no account [to] manufacture any warlike weapons . . . but confine yourself exclusively to the making of Agricultural Implements, Fishing Tackle and such Articles, as are employed in the peaceful arts.*

The New Zealanders had other ideas, and Kemp was forced to mend their guns and cast bullets for them, skills they learned rapidly.

To make sufficient agricultural articles to trade for provisions was impossible as Kemp was explaining by September 1820 '1st because I cannot make these so well to their minds as the English are made' and secondly because his time was taken up with building. He did however manage during the first months to make parts for the plough and harrow, a crab for landing timber and some cramps for binding the shingles for the house he and Francis Hall were building. This house had been begun in January 1820, the blacksmith's shop being neither wind nor watertight, with the Kemps' bed 'literally rotten with damp'. The house, though unfinished, could be moved into in August 1820 and was considered by the missionaries to be the first 'permanent' dwelling at Kerikeri. The blacksmith's shop then became a temporary chapel and did double duty as a barn for a time. More ground was cleared in front of the house, grass seed sown and a new paling fence put up to enclose the whole.

Although the Kemps and Francis Hall were more comfortable physically in their new home, the prospect of being driven from the settlement filled their minds, despite Marsden's presence in New Zealand and his encouragement. The New Zealanders, wrote Francis Hall, 'would scruple not to tell them' constantly, that if they would not supply them with muskets and powder they had better go away. The Kerikeri mission was experiencing the same problems which had beset the Rangihoua brethren over the years since 1815. The Rev. John Butler as Superintendent had managed at first to avoid taking part in the forbidden trade, but once even he was forced to barter half a musket and some powder. The employees of the missions, however, appear to have had no qualms at all and would, to the horror of the missionaries, even trade on Sunday. The whaleboats from the ships were coming with increasing frequency to Kerikeri, aided by those at Rangihoua, the sailors travelling further inland to Waimate and even to the Hokianga in their search to buy pigs. Not only did this trade deprive the mission of essential fresh meat, but this 'moral pestilence' as Francis Hall called the whalers, spread disease amongst the New Zealanders.

The mission was sorely tried by the New Zealanders too, who took fencing day after day for firewood, trampled the wheat and 'insulted' them, but it was the scenes around the New Zealanders' village at Kerikeri which sickened their sensibilities. Slaves died of hunger and were eaten by the dogs, or, if caught in an attempt to steal food, were dispatched with a blow of a mere, cooked in the umu and eaten. Shrieks from the nearby village drew the brethren from their houses one moonlit night. Helpless to intervene, they were witness to a woman being 'cruelly used' by the

Chief Moka, while others of the tribe stood around 'enjoying the lustful scene'. He would have been hung in England, wrote Francis Hall in revulsion. The evangelism which they trusted would wean the New Zealanders away from what the missionaries perceived as cruel and heathenish practices was making no ground.

What the brethren saw as the turbulent and provocative behaviour of the New Zealanders towards the missions did nothing to unite the missionaries. Tensions between individuals had been apparent since the early days at Rangihoua, and now the presence of John Butler as Superintendent of both stations aggravated their grievances. Butler was later to be termed hasty and injudicious, warm in his temper and unstable, and was disliked by all at both settlements. Even the mild James Kemp and Francis Hall were often in conflict with him over what now appear petty, but to them were arrogant and hurtful, actions. Butler's acts were to be the main reasons later for Francis Hall's leaving New Zealand and Shepherd's retreat to Whangaroa. Bean and Fairburn, the carpenters at Kerikeri, refused to be dominated by him, and Mrs Butler suffered from the rude and ugly behaviour of the labourers who would not take his orders. His stay at Rangihoua in 1819 had resulted in violent altercations with Thomas Kendall who declared that he would not acknowledge any man for his master in New Zealand.

This unhappy and alienated man had been alarmed and angry when Kendall had left to go to England in March 1820, taking with him the chief Waikato and the protector of the Kerikeri mission, Hongi Hika. Marsden protested that nothing short of violence, which he had neither the authority or inclination to exercise, would have retained Kendall in New Zealand. Kendall was set on persuading the Church Missionary Society in London that he be ordained, ostensibly to be a more useful instrument of the Society amongst the New Zealanders, but the truth was that without ordination he would remain subject to the orders of his adversary, the Rev. John Butler.

In fact, while Kendall was away, Marsden had remarked that he thought Butler's habits were too deeply rooted ever to change and although he might succeed as a minister, his obstinacy and strong passions made him unsuitable in the management of public concerns and of his subordinates. For, wrote Marsden, although Mrs Butler had never wished to come to New Zealand and this would have unsettled her husband's mind, Butler's own severity of expression was 'unpleasant to those who have not been accustomed to that mode of Address'.

The New Zealanders had first hand observation of the quarrelsome community and must have noted Butler's inability to control even the mechanics who refused to do his bidding. Marsden at last asked him what authority he wished to maintain. Butler, ground down by his responsibility and the resentment of the brethren, felt for his own comfort and peace of mind that he must resign from his position as Superintendent. Francis Hall was then given control of the stores, appointed secretary for meetings and superintendent of both the lay settlers and mechanics on a temporary basis. Butler felt that if he were to be confined only to his minister's duties and his farming he would need a home worthy of his status. Thus it came about that all his energies were directed towards the building of the Mission House. The story of the building of this house and of its occupants, until it passed into the private ownership of James Kemp in 1860, is told in Section 1 of Part II of this book.

Chapter 4

Troubled Years
1820–1821

During the troubled year of 1820, on 29 March, Richard Alexander Fairburn had been born to the wife of the carpenter, William Fairburn, the first Pakeha child to be born at Kerikeri. He was probably born in the Fairburn's quarters in the settlement storehouse. These quarters in 1821 had been floored, and a ceiling now created loft spaces in the gabled roofs reached by stepladders from each of the 'apartments'. Shutters closed the settlers' windows and iron bars protected those spaces where the stores were housed. As the partitions in the store separated the Bean, Puckey, Fairburn and Butler families, so interior fences divided the area within the high paling fence which surrounded the temporary chapel (the old blacksmith's shop) the new Hall/Kemp house and the storehouse into private spaces for gardens and outhouses.

Butler's large kitchen-outhouse was being built near the Kerikeri River in November 1820 when Marsden, James Shepherd, William Puckey Snr and John Butler set off in the Kerikeri mission's whaleboat to the Firth of Thames where the government ship *Coromandel* was collecting a cargo of spars. Shepherd had a flair for the Maori language (unlike Butler, Hall and Kemp) and William Puckey Snr was an experienced navigator. At the Thames they visited the Ngati Maru chief Hinaki's pa at Mokoia (Panmure, Auckland) and ventured up the Waitemata, crossing overland to the Kaipara Harbour, from where Marsden and Shepherd returned on foot to the Bay of Islands. Butler and Puckey returned to Mokoia and from there sailed back in the whaleboat to Kerikeri. While at Mokoia on the return, Butler had accepted the gift of the island of Motu Ihe (now part of the Hauraki Gulf Maritime Park).

Still smarting from having to relinquish the superintendency of the missions, Butler now saw a possible way to escape his unhappy position at

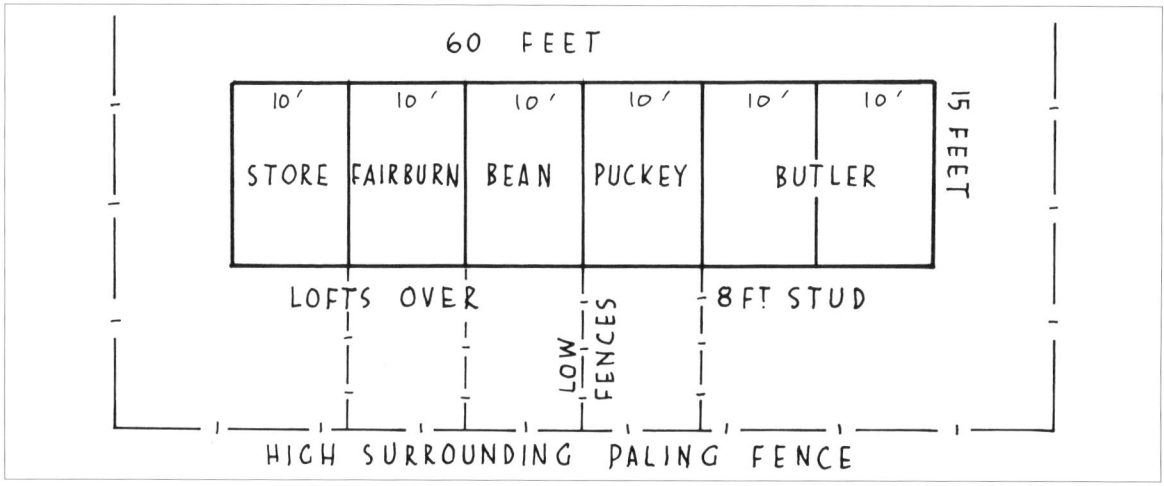

Plan of the store, in the year 1821, showing the possible layout of the 'apartments' occupied by missionaries, lay people and their families. The positions of the Butler's two rooms and the Puckey's single room are known.

Kerikeri. In December 1820, on the point of Marsden's departure from New Zealand after ten months' stay, Butler proposed to Marsden that he should form a new mission station at Mokoia. Cattle would be safe on Motu Ihe Island and if the Society would send him a good quadrant and nautical almanac he would be able to make a general survey of the 'Inhabitants, Productions, Timber, Harbours, Lakes, Rivers, Minerals, etc.' Marsden told Butler he could make a trial if he must, but without the Society's sanction a large expenditure of stores would not be allowed. The act would be upon Butler's own head if he was not prepared to wait for the approval of the Society. Marsden did not seem to have been totally averse to the idea. However, the Wesleyan, the Rev. Samuel Leigh, planning in New South Wales to start a Wesleyan mission in New Zealand, thought that the Waitemata Harbour could be the ideal place. The gift of Mokoia was much discussed by the Corresponding Committee in New South Wales, and Butler was accused, unjustly, by some members of acquiring it for himself.

Once settled back at Kerikeri, Butler appears to have changed his mind almost immediately, becoming absorbed with his plans for his house and his agricultural activities. Gardening and the growing of grain was something he had his heart in and was good at. There was wheat to reap from the first ploughing and planting of 1820 and the first sickle was put into the wheat on 14 December. Everyone went to reap at Kerikeri and then to gather the crop which James Shepherd had planted at Okura. This first bountiful harvest was stowed in the loft of the temporary chapel, an aromatic accompaniment to their thankful prayers. But even while they worked and prayed together, the bitter feelings surfaced when Butler appropriated a large piece of canvas for a threshing floor for his wheat, there being no barn to thresh in. This upset the storekeeper Francis Hall, for now dust and rubbish fell into the room below through the cracks in the ceiling where before the canvas had been spread as protection. This seemingly trivial matter was to them important and another source of discord.

The mission was very short of food again, being out of tea, sugar and flour. Five ships were at the Bay and were like 'the Locust in the land of Egypt' buying up all the pigs. Marsden had promised to send salt meat, and anxious watch was kept from the heights above Kerikeri for the arrival of the *Active* at Paroa Bay, beyond the point at Kororareka (Russell). Fishing with a seine net was tried down the inlet without success.

The effect of the privations on the women of the mission, almost yearly pregnant, is a matter for speculation, but birth itself was hazardous even for the hardiest. When Mrs Kemp's second child (the first had been stillborn after their arrival at Rangihoua in August 1819) was being born at Kerikeri in January 1821, she was extremely ill. Francis Hall chased all about the Bay to find a ship's surgeon who would come to her aid, finally securing the services of Mr McCurdy of the *Seringapatum* lying in Paroa Bay. Henry Tacy Kemp was safely delivered, and to the great relief of all the *Active* arrived with the vital supplies.

The New Zealanders, stocked up with muskets and powder from the visiting ships, were oblivious to the mission concerns, and in this same month Rewa and his warriors went off to fight to the southward at Mercury Bay. As always, the elevated passions of the tribe preparing for war overflowed into 'teasing of the settlers'. The New Zealanders' slaves suffered too. Francis Hall finding an emaciated girl slave near death in the bracken being pelted with stones and tortured by some boys, was helpless to assist, except to bury her later in a fern-strewn grave rather than leave her to be eaten by dogs. For this, an act of decency in his eyes, Francis Hall was ridiculed, abused with 'indecent' language and had a stone thrown at him as he sat at the door of his house.

With the warriors gone by the end of February 1821, the mission breathed a little more easily and in March the Butlers' son Samuel together with James Shepherd, his new wife Harriet (a widow), and the bullock man from the 1820 *Dromedary* visit, John Lee, returned to New Zealand. The Rev. John Butler had been unable to control his son when they had stayed on arrival in 1819 at Rangihoua, and Sam had been returned to Parramatta in New South Wales to be under Marsden's watchful eye. Now he was to enquire into the manufacture of New Zealand flax. Shepherd as a missionary settler was to visit native settlements, travel with the chiefs on their war expeditions as an observer and to plant at Okura, his old camp, an acre of flax varieties with the idea of establishing a rope walk. Shepherd was the only one of the Kerikeri settlers with any grasp of the native language, and this above all, he was told, should be his prime object — the acquisition and writing of the language. The Shepherds moved in for the time being with the Kemps and Francis Hall while John Lee and Sam Butler joined the Butlers in their rooms in the storehouse.

John Butler had earlier hoped his son would be going to Okura, but now he proposed setting up a new mission station at Te Tii at the head of the Te Puna Inlet in the Ngati Rehia chief Tareha's domain. Five to six acres were bought for two hatchets, two axes, two hoes and six adzes, and in honour of the British sovereign named 'King George Farm'. The chief Tareha was renowned for his great stature and ferocity and was a thorn in the sides of the missionaries when he passed through Kerikeri on his way to Waimate where he maintained his tribal interests. Butler called him 'our great chief' seeming to rate his status and influence above that of Hongi Hika or Rewa. Butler may have been using Tareha to extend his influence through his son, away from Kerikeri. Equally, Tareha was using Butler in his quest for firearms. A mission established in his territory at Te Tii, where he was the only ariki, would bring the ships' boats to trade, and his mana would increase. One musket it was said was worth seventy baskets of potatoes and two pigs.

In 1821 the missionaries at Kerikeri were living up to the agreement made with Marsden the previous year not to trade in muskets. Their employees were not and the missionary journals record that the carpenters were paying so much for pigs as they saw, it was said, the Rangihoua missionaries trading in muskets, and determined to do likewise. Mission cattle as a source of fresh meat was not yet available to them, and were in any case roaming, with no fences to restrain them, from Kahikatearoa to the Waipapa. More than once utu, in mission goods, was demanded by and given to the tribes on whose plantations the animals had trampled. Each of the missionaries had a cow with calf at foot in the settlement as a source of milk and butter, and these were turned out with the main herd across the Kerikeri River about April. In 1821 the herd was twenty-seven strong when rounded up, and doing well on the native grasses.

John Lee, the bullocky, had not broken any of the cattle to harness for the plough in time for the wheat planting in May. The reason, he contended, was that his time had been spent at Kahikatearoa cutting timber for John Butler's house. The plough could not be used and the wheat was dibbled, the seeds being sown singly by hand in the burnt-over ground. Despite all their efforts, the Kerikeri Mission would never be self-sufficient in food.

The comparative peace of the mission in 1821, planting and building, was disturbed at times by the return or setting out of the New Zealanders' war expeditions. Rewa, Wharepapa and Hauraki, who had left in February, returned through Kerikeri in April. Tareha who was in dispute with a Hokianga hapu caused some upsets, and Te Morenga returned to Okura with 'heads alive' and went inland to kill and eat them. The Kerikeri people wanted revenge on the Okura people for stealing a pig. Charles Hongi, the eldest son of Hongi Hika, was badly burned by gunpowder exploding (a not uncommon happening) and was brought to Kerikeri on a stretcher where the brethren tended him.

But the most disturbing events were yet to happen with the return of Hongi Hika, Waikato and Thomas Kendall from England to the Bay of Islands.

Chapter 5

Hongi Hika's Return
1821

On Friday 13 July 1821, Hongi Hika came to Kerikeri and the peace of the mission was destroyed. Fences were again taken, gardens robbed, and the ships' crews coming up to Kerikeri were stripped of goods. Kemp, who had earlier refused the requests of the New Zealanders to mend their muskets, had to vacate his blacksmith's shop, where they now cast musket balls and used his tools to mend their guns. Charles Hongi was again wounded, this time by the recoil of a pistol. Plans for building Rewa a European style house — he had been 'good' the eighteen months Hongi had been absent — were set aside.

Hongi had arrived back in Sydney unwell and Marsden wrote that he also had found 'Hongi's mind a little hurt from being refused some things that he wanted'. Hongi Hika's mind had been more than a little hurt. He had been insulted. He told his tribe that after all the missionaries were but 'Cooks', that King George who had given him an audience had known nothing of them, not even of the Rev. Samuel Marsden. Before he had gone to England he had been refused the grey horse (brought down by the *Dromedary*). Other chiefs had been given a piece of red cloth (red was a chiefly symbol) but he had not. Also Marsden and Butler had written letters which caused him to be badly received at Missionary House in London. There he had only been given at first £25 worth of ironmongery, whereas Toi and Tetere of the enemy tribe Ngaere Raumati, lesser people, had been given far more on their visit. Noting Hongi's outrage, the Church Missionary Society had reconsidered and later gave him more ironmongery, two suits of clothes and two watches amounting to about £80 worth and recorded:

That the same is approved, in acknowledgement of the protection afforded by

> *Shunghee to the Settlers in the Bay of Islands, and of a Grant by him of a large Tract of Land to the Society for the small consideration of 40 axes.*

Not that this placatory gesture altered Hongi's feelings towards those at Missionary House. These were only some of the many gifts he received while in England, which were largely turned into muskets when he arrived in Sydney. To add to his injured state of mind, on his return to Kerikeri he learned of

> *some ill language which Mr Puckey's children and perhaps the parents too made use of with respect to Shunghee in his absence saying he was not a very great Rangateeda and that they should boil him in a pot on his return.*

The chief's person being absolutely tapu, Puckey was attacked. James Kemp recorded:

> *. . . eirly in the morning, three or four of the Neighbouring Natives; broke into the house of Wm Puckeys the Carpenters; and one of them took his son; that was sleeping at a short distance, [the outside kitchen] by the hair of his head, and said if you spake I will cut your head off; and stool a number of articles.*

Blankets, razors, shoes, plates, clothes were taken — even the bread that was baking in a pan. Butler suffered too from a party who rushed into his garden where his house was being built and stole tools and tore down fencing.

Hongi had learned, perhaps from his old enemy Hinaki of Mokoia (Ngati Maru tribe) whom he had confronted in Sydney with the promise that he would wreak revenge on this tribe on his return to New Zealand, that Butler had been given Motu Ihe Island and that he would be going to live there. Perhaps this seemed a good idea to Hongi, for with the hated Butler gone his friend Kendall could come to Kerikeri. But Rewa said 'No, no, if you turn him off your land he shall then live on mine'. Rewa had stood up for the settlers in the Puckey affair. But like the other chiefs at Kerikeri he tolerated the settlers for the advantages to be had and later even he burst into the 'church' during a service to say he would no longer be their great friend unless he was given a gun.

Butler had given Rewa the coveted red cloth, to Hongi's mortification. Now, the perceptive Francis Hall presented the irate Hongi with a square of scarlet cloth, and noted that it was the first time that Hongi's mind had been at rest since his return. But the attacks on the ship's boats coming to Kerikeri continued, more threats were made to Puckey and Butler and the New Zealanders continued to cast balls in Kemp's blacksmiths shop. Hall wrote, 'the poor Women in the Family way are sadly alarmed . . . All are thinking of leaving the first Opportunity'. The day after Francis Hall wrote this, a daughter was born to Mrs Fairburn.

By September 1821, when the taua was ready to leave for the south to make war against the Ngati Paoa and their allies, Ngati Maru, Hongi's 'Fury and malice' seemed somewhat abated. The morning of departure, the 'Large beautiful Canoes' with seventy warriors in each were exercised up and down the Inlet to show their style, with Hongi dressed in the scarlet uniform given him in England. In the afternoon they left to join with Te Morenga, differences cast aside, and other tribes who came from Hokianga, to go against their common enemy, the Ngati Maru of the Firth of Thames. It was said that 2000 men with 1000 muskets left the Bay. Down the Kerikeri Inlet the mission cattle were shot at, and the mission salt works in Manawaora Bay were destroyed for the second time.

Although the missionaries held Thomas Kendall largely responsible for Hongi's attitude to them, Francis Hall and James Kemp mixed sympathy with disapproval in their friendship with Kendall. They agreed with the Rev. Thomas Kendall's criticisms of Marsden as the Church Missionary Society agent. He had sent inadequate supplies from New South Wales (his 'sow or starve' policy) and all felt that he ignored their very real difficulties. Kendall had written

> *Shunghee is a good man for a savage barbarian; and he is disposed to be a friend to us as much as ever. But then he would be an enemy to us if we opposed his interest (taking them according to his own views), however we might conscientiously disapprove of promoting them.*

He wrote also that the missionaries needed praise for their efforts, not be crushed by being condemned for the little they were able to do. The mild, pious and prudent Francis Hall added a footnote to Kendall's letter: 'The letter takes so just a view of the difficulties we have to contend with . . .'. The New Zealanders dictated the terms of trade. The moral reasons behind the refusal of the missionaries to trade in muskets were not understood and their reluctance was seen as obstinacy.

Kendall's letter was read at the first quarterly meeting of the missionaries in New Zealand on 27 August 1821, and it was decided, in view of the unsettled climate, that plans for new mission stations at Hokianga, Whangaroa and Thames be postponed. John Butler at this meeting also announced his intention of visiting New South Wales. His declared motive was to challenge Marsden for his neglect and procure food supplies for the mission. On 27 November 1821, Butler sailed, accompanied by Mrs Bean, Mrs Fairburn and their children, Susannah Kendall, Thomas Foster, the blacksmith from Rangihoua, and that drunken pair John Lee, the bullock man, and James Boyle, the salt man.

The manner of Butler's challenge to Marsden was to lead to his downfall. An angry Marsden wrote to Francis Hall of his having to endure much bad language from Butler. Never in his life had he been spoken to in that way. 'If the Rev. Mr Butler means what he says, he will not be long with you' he added ominously. Marsden would have to wait upon the approval of any action against Butler from the Church Missionary Society. It took well over a year before he had the necessary authority in hand. By then Butler's removal would be no simple matter.

Meanwhile, Francis Hall, Samuel Butler, Bean and William Fairburn, Mr and Mrs Kemp, Mr and Mrs Shepherd and Mrs Butler held the fort at Kerikeri for the three months John Butler was away. On 4 December Mrs Shepherd had her first child. It was during this time that events took place which the missionaries declared were the most horrifying they had ever witnessed.

Chapter 6

The New Zealanders' Customs
1821–1823

On 19 December 1821, the war canoes began to return triumphant from their battle with the Ngati Maru at Mokoia. First came those of Muriwai's tribe, 200 in three canoes. Half were prisoners of war 'weeping and mourning bitterly'. With their captives the tribe set off on the long trek to their villages on the Hokianga Harbour. With them had come the news of the deaths of Tete (Hongi's son-in-law) and of Tete's brother at the Mokoia affray.

Two days later the Waimate tribes returned and the men of the mission went to the Wairoa Stream to see the ceremony of their landing. James Kemp recorded the scene

> . . . *a number of native came out of their Canoes and began to dance and sing their war song and as they danced they lifted up into the air a number of heads which they had killed and taken in war. And as a mark of disgrace on the English thes[e] heads are bought by the Ships that touch here for Gunpowder: this is one thing which causes the natives to have such a low opinion of us. After the natives had finished dancing a canoe came in sight having therein two dead bodies that were killed in the fight they were brothers one of them . . . was a very kind and industrious man more so than any other at our Settlement [Tete] . . . as soon as the canoes came close to the Shore the Wife and friends of Tettee immediately seised three of the Slaves and draged [sic] them into the water and destroyed them in a most cruel manner this scene was so distressing to our feelings that we all returned to our houses . . . The next morning myself and Mr Shephard went to speak to Shunghee when we saw them roasting human flesh Shunghee said it was very good . . .*

Kemp and Hall had been greatly distressed to see 'Koshaddei', who lived in their home and cared for the Kemp's baby, help to kill two of the slaves.

She 'is not coming back to us again' wrote an appalled Francis Hall. Further, Hongi offered them some cooked human flesh. The missionaries tried in their halting Maori to impress on Hongi 'how exceedingly sinful it was in the sight of God' but

> *they made light of what we said and answered it was very good for New Zealand man . . . the Native spirit is reviving . . . They are again preparing for another fighting expedition and are very teasing for me to mend their muskets and I am obliged to comply with a great many of their requests though very much against my will . . . I cannot see it my duty to remain here when obliged to comply with things so contrary to the objects of the Society.*

Kemp wrote this in January 1822, and Francis Hall wrote the same month in fear and faith

> *If I am killed and eaten by these ferocious men I know that Jesus will find my poor body at the last trump whether it be put in a grave or a New Zealander's belly.*

The New Zealanders met the horror and disgust of the missionaries with amused derision. This way was New Zealand man's way: to fight, to avenge — it was his reason for being. They were proud of their triumph at the Thames and expected the missionaries to be pleased to hear about it. Hongi, wrote Marsden, had justly observed to him

> *that we have made no new laws, we have established no new custom; we are only following the institutions of our forefathers, which we cannot as yet relinquish . . .*

Marsden commented

> *We do not abhor their cannabilism more than they abhor our custom of hanging felons . . . they think it better to kill a man with one blow than hang him. We do not see the New Zealanders drinking and swearing and murdering one another, as is the case in civil society.*

As a mark of victory Hongi was tattooed afresh upon his thigh and came to the mission to have these wounds dressed. Tete's widow in her sorrow, and as was customary, tried to do away with herself. First she shot herself, and only being wounded, tried unsuccessfully to starve herself to death.

Two months after the warriors returned, in February 1822, the canoes were again dropping down the Kerikeri Inlet to rendezvous at Rangihoua 'to form one of the greatest armaments which has ever taken place in New Zealand' before setting out on another voyage of vengeance southward. At Kerikeri several hundreds from a distance had encamped on the hills around the settlement — 'the din which they make is dreadful'. Into this turmoil came John Butler, back from New South Wales.

At this time the missionaries were confronted with the strongest of all tapu, that connected with death. The bodies of Tete and Apu had been entombed by the river. Under threat of having their houses or the boat broken, or even of death, should they pass the sacred place on Kororipo Point, the missionaries were forced to carry the goods overland from below the Wairoa and utu was extracted by various chiefs. When on 27 February 1827, 1000 warriors left Kerikeri to join 2000 more at Rangihoua, the departing forces stripped the mission gardens of pumpkin, lettuces and cabbage to add to their supplies. Both the Kemps had been brought to their beds of a 'nervous disorder' in February as a consequence of all the alarming events. With the warriors gone, some tranquillity might have been expected. Instead, with the return of John Butler in this same month, the internal divisions within the small community created further tensions. Butler had returned with a great quantity of goods which he would not put in the charge of Francis Hall who was storekeeper. Hall had received Marsden's irate letter threatening Butler's dismissal and now wrote despairingly to Marsden,

> *He has returned the same Mr Butler as he was when he went . . . May God Almighty in mercy change his crooked disposition and make him an useful instrument*

but offered Marsden the solace that he, Marsden, stood 'on too high ground to be reached by his pygmy shafts'. To the Society he wrote begging them to overlook Marsden's faults and magnify his fame.

Hall was grieved too by the expressions of 'that forward young man Saml. Butler'. Sam took off on 'a party of pleasure' with the carpenters on the Sabbath — 'may the Lord in mercy teach these poor men to know themselves better.' One of the carpenters, it was later said, had given a New Zealand girl venereal disease. It was also rumoured that the Okura tribe might give Shepherd's plot of land there to Sam Butler, Sam having enjoyed the favours of a lady of that tribe. This rumour brought an accusation against Shepherd who was said to have shown the same favours to another Okura girl. Indeed, wrote Butler, Mrs Butler had said that every man in the mission had been 'carnally connected' with New Zealand women. Francis Hall protested that although opportunities had not been wanting his 'Dear Lord' had preserved him from folly. Butler's accusation in defence of his son Sam Butler, was certainly extravagant. He would later admit that as a single man Sam had transgressed, but that further accusations were malicious — that is, after Sam had married. At this time it seemed a good idea to pack Sam off to New South Wales to seek a wife, and in May 1822, he embarked on the *Vansittart* with the returning carpenters Bean and Fairburn.

It seemed to be the season of illicit relationships, the Rev. Thomas Kendall horrifying his colleagues when his affair with his New Zealand servant girl Tungaroa in the first months of 1822 reached their ears. This was of much more serious concern as Kendall continued to administer the sacraments. All these transgressions duly came to the notice of the Society. By September 1822 it had passed resolutions to admonish Butler, who would need to manifest a more Christian temper if he was to be of further service to the mission. Kendall was to be dismissed. By February 1823 the Society had resolved to dismiss Sam Butler and his father, but at the next meeting rescinded Butler's dismissal, instead requiring John Butler to make 'an unequivocal confession of his sorrow for the same to Mr Marsden'. His future good conduct would confirm the sincerity of his repentance but he should leave the New Zealand mission. When Marsden came to the Bay of Islands armed with the sanctions of the Society in August 1823 he was aware that, though desirable, it would be no easy task to put these resolutions into practice.

In the interval, however, it seems that Butler had never felt more secure. He had his house. He issued goods as he wished, mostly without reference to Francis Hall, and his large barn built at the end of 1822 secured his grain harvest. Thomas Hansen had come up from Rangihoua to break in the bullocks for the plough. Shepherd did not return to Okura but renovated the Butlers' former rooms in the store for his family's use, while the carpenter Puckey expanded into Bean and Fairburn's former rooms with his family. The New Zealanders' village on the hill was quiet. Rumours of attack by the Kaipara tribes drove the defenceless remnant left at Kerikeri to hide at times in the bush at night over the months the warriors were away.

The triumphant taua, with the chiefs Rewa, Moka and Hongi returned to their seaport of Wairoa in July 1822 with many prisoners of war. The sounds which came to the settlers of wives crying, and slaves moaning were reminiscent of December 1821, but this time the missionaries did not venture to see the returning warriors. There was a report of two prisoners killed and eaten. Hongi was jubilant. In the Waikato 1500 had been killed and in celebration of this latest triumph his face was tattooed afresh. Sore from these facial wounds, but in genial mood he brought the settlers gifts of kumara and pigeons. Yet, according to the chief Te Morenga, the slaughter in the Waikato went against custom. Before the northern tribes had muskets, if, during a battle, two chiefs of consequence were killed, peace was made. Now whole tribes were cut off. The chief Moka, however, was of the opinion that tomahawks were more

effective weapons. He had killed forty with a tomahawk and only five with his gun.

The ceremonial of lifting the tapu from the returned warriors completed, the menfolk returned to their homes and wives. Here the scenes were not always ones of rejoicing, for the men had brought with them slave wives. Gregory had brought two fine women from Waikato. His jealous head wife gave him a good thrashing and broke his gun.

A few weeks later, sad lamentations were heard all night from the Wairoa Stream and the missionaries found the New Zealanders gathered around a canoe which had overturned, two occupants having drowned. The tapu canoe would never be used again, but, drawn on to the bank, would be left to rot. This canoe may have been the one the remains of

War canoe of New Zealand. From Dumont d'Urville's Voyage Pittoresque Autour du Monde.
AUCKLAND INSTITUTE AND MUSEUM

which were still on the Wairoa Stream early this century. Like almost every other article found later about Kerikeri, it was then said to have been Hongi Hika's. In the same way the Kororipo Pa site is said to have been Hongi Hika's fortified pa, but it is quite clear that Kororipo had ceased to be a stronghold by this time.

The New Zealanders' village and the settlement remained relatively quiet for the rest of 1822, although on one occasion Rewa, on being refused permission to store potatoes at Puckey's place, became so enraged that he threatened to take the mission goods away and gathered up the tools lying about. Fortunately the threat went no further. The New Zealanders were as much concerned with their own politics as the missionaries were with the scandalous behaviour of Kendall and its implications for the Kerikeri Mission Station. Suspended from missionary service from the middle of the year, the unhappy Kendall, who had fled to Hokianga was, by the end of that year, speaking wildly of coming to Kerikeri. The alarmed missionaries foresaw that, should Hongi achieve his wish to have Kendall at Kerikeri, the deep-rooted hatred of both Kendall and Hongi for Butler would lead to the abandonment of the settlement. Their condemnation of Kendall's behaviour was tempered by their affection and pity for the man. Indeed, Shepherd was to write, 'I wish we had all acted more Christian like to Mr Kendall than we have done.' There was no doubt they would rather have had him with them as their minister than the Rev. John Butler. James Kemp wrote to Kendall with love from all their family, and in the hope that the Lord would support and uphold him, enabling him 'to proclaim to the poor perishing heathen.'

Francis Hall left this troubled settlement for good on 3 December 1822. On this day he took his last walk in the brethren's company around the gardens, and after breakfast and prayers they parted with tears. Although Francis Hall had prayed fervently that his Lord would be pleased to carry him back to his native land, with human perversity, after a year back in England he was making fruitless efforts to return to New Zealand.

Hall's departure left the Butlers, Kemps, Shepherds and Puckeys at the mission. Francis Hall was to inform the Church Missionary Society in London on his return, that Shepherd was 'getting on very quickly in the New Zealand language', had translated hymns, and had begun on the Gospel of St John. 'He is a clever young man (but I hope he will not think more of himself on that account)'. William Puckey Jnr, about sixteen or seventeen years old and now employed by the mission, he wished to be encouraged 'as he speaks the language as well as the natives' and suggested that under a clergyman he might become a 'very clever School Master'. (This he did become later, founding, with Joseph Matthews, the Kaitaia Mission in 1834.) As to Kemp, Hall told the Society it could place every confidence in him — a 'pious, admirable, judicious' man. He confirmed his former views on John Butler and Puckey Snr.

January 1823 saw the harvest being reaped again and stored in the large barn newly built for Butler. Shepherd and Kemp had begun the first school for the New Zealanders since the station was founded at Kerikeri, and were collecting timber to begin a school/chapel building. Kendall, now living at Matauwhi Bay near Kororareka, came to visit both the sympathetic Kemp and his friend Hongi, reviving Butler's fears that with Hongi's continued antipathy towards himself, Kendall would come to live at Kerikeri. But Hongi and his warriors left again for war in February 1823 for the East Cape and Rotorua, and Thomas Kendall remained at Kororareka.

In New South Wales, Samuel Marsden was planning to come to New Zealand bringing with him the Rev. Henry Williams and his family to settle them at Whangaroa. A total change was promised the New Zealand mission. Kendall's dismissal was certain, but early in 1823 Marsden wrote to the Rev. John Butler in an attempt at reconciliation as the Church Missionary Society had recommended. He still had need of Butler for the time being. Butler replied that he too was willing to forget past differences.

The cry of the New Zealanders to have a missionary at their settlements was increasing. Tareha seemed determined to have a missionary in his territory. Sam Butler was due to return soon, and anticipating the placing of his son under Tareha's protection, Butler went to have a look at likely places at Takou Bay and the Mangonui Inlet. 'Tareha' he wrote, 'is peculiarly attached to my son Samuel'. Moreover Tareha's influence being paramount in this area, a mission station there would not be subject to the vagaries of many chiefs as had happened at Kerikeri.

Sam Butler returned to Kerikeri with his new bride in 1823. James Shepherd, already unhappy at what he felt were attempts by John Butler to thwart his efforts to build a school, was in a dilemma. His letters to the Church Missionary Society had been most vehement in their condemnation of both Butlers — father and son. He must have known that his reports on Sam Butler's fornication at Okura would result in the younger Butler's dismissal. The prospect of being the object of their united anger so lowered his spirits, that he determined to accompany the Wesleyans who were to begin a mission at Whangaroa, and settle there with them.

The Wesleyans' first choice of the Mokoia Pa area of Tamaki had been abandoned. Hongi had forbidden it in 1821 when he intended to fight there. Whangarei was their second proposal, but here they found that the population had either been killed or had left. They chose Whangaroa where Marsden had thought Henry Williams might go. In June 1823, gathering seeds, plants, cuttings and poultry together at Kerikeri, John Butler and the Shepherds accompanied the Wesleyans to Whangaroa. Butler after three weeks returned to Kerikeri, while Shepherd with his wife and child stayed on.

Marsden arrived in the Bay with the Williams family and the returning Fairburn family in August 1823. With the Wesleyans now at Whangaroa, the Rev. Henry Williams began building his station at Paihia. Shepherd was brought back into the fold from Whangaroa by the sympathetic Marsden, and plans were made to settle him at Parengaroa near the Waipapa Estuary, a few miles down the north side of the inlet from

Kerikeri. This move was mainly to placate the chief 'Towee' who was upset that Henry Williams was not to be with him. 'Towee' had also been angry at Shepherd's going to Whangaroa and at Kendall for seducing Tungaroa, tapu to Towee as a wife. Persuaded by Marsden, 'Towee' began to build Shepherd a raupo house at Parengaroa, despite the fact that in their eyes he had only lately been transformed from slave to gentleman in being made a member of the missionary committee.

A raupo house was being built for the Williams at Paihia while Mrs Williams and her children stayed with the Butlers at Kerikeri. Mrs Butler, wrote Marianne Williams, had 'received us in a manner as kind as it was blunt', and moreover 'Mr and Mrs Butler were hospitably kind with no lack of good cheer and English bottled porter'.

With the fighting men absent 'the missionaries could stroll out of their high paled yards and gardens in perfect quiet'. Mrs Williams with her three children often went to visit Mrs Kemp in the house near the store, whom she 'felt to love as a sister' at the first interview. The Kemp's pretty house was pronounced as 'neat as wax'; having been freshly whitewashed inside and out in the previous month. Mrs Kemp had in the house 'three very pleasing-looking New Zealand girls, tidily dressed, in English bedgowns and aprons' who welcomed her with 'a courtesy', and 'How do you do, Ma'am?' in answer to her 'Te na ra ca coe?'. Of the New Zealand women she wrote that they were 'some of them very stout, and not very tall'. The New Zealand women said of them 'Mr Williams is very good, the tamaities, children, very good. But Mrs Williams is too long, and not stout enough', or as Jane said, 'not big enough round the shoulders and waist, like Mrs Butler and Mrs Leigh'.

With Marsden had also come a ticket of leave convict William Spickman to join the mission as a herdsman. A conscientious and capable man, he was to be of great help to the mission for many years at Kerikeri and later at Waimate. He eventually settled at Whangaroa where some descendants live today.

The arrangement put in hand by John Butler for Samuel Butler to start a settlement at Te Tii (or the Mangonui Inlet — Tareha's River) received Marsden's qualified approval. Shepherd would be going to Parengaroa. James Kemp was to take charge of the cattle with the help of Spickman (until the promised farmer Davis would arrive) and a stockyard across the Kerikeri River from Butler's house was being enclosed, the first enclosure to be made for the roaming cattle. The Shepherds in the meantime returned to their old lodgings in the store. James Shepherd took up his shoemaking again and composed another hymn or two to add to those which had so pleased Marianne Williams when the New Zealanders sang them for her on board the ship *Brampton* when they had first arrived.

Kendall's case was now considered by the committee of missionaries under the chairmanship of Marsden. The broken Kendall finally agreed to leave, as also did Cowell of Rangihoua. The Wesleyan, the Rev. Samuel Leigh, who was very ill, was to leave New Zealand too, with Marsden on the *Brampton*. Despite the Captain of the *Brampton*'s assurance to Mrs Williams that 'Sunday's sail will never fail' the *Brampton* was wrecked in a storm on Brampton Reef not far from the mouth of the Kerikeri Inlet. Marsden and the distressed Leighs came back to Kerikeri.

Everything was now changed. Rewa, arriving back at Kerikeri told Marsden that if Kendall went away 'Shunghee would cry much and be very angry.' Hongi came back to Waimate, and with his return Marsden was in a quandary. Kendall now refused to leave New Zealand and should Hongi support him and bring him to Kerikeri it would be impossible for John Butler to stay.

Butler and his son were already setting out Samuel's house at Te Tii. Marsden objected to the size of this dwelling. No timber in any case was to be used for mission buildings — a school for the New Zealanders, he ordered, must be built first, and also a house for Hongi which had been promised to him years before. Marsden was perhaps alarmed that Kendall, if he came to Kerikeri, might build one for Hongi first.

Hongi had told Marsden that he would now turn his attention to agriculture instead of war and would perhaps build a road from Kerikeri to his cultivations at Waimate. Marsden gave several gifts to Hongi of clothing. Seeing Hongi at one time 'sitting down with a large needle and twine sewing up the cracks in the soles of his feet' he suggested to the missionaries that gifts such as shoes were a way of 'gaining the esteem of the chiefs by a little well-timed attention and at little expense'. Marsden needed to gain Hongi's favour with the ever-present threat of Kendall looming — but shoes and clothing would not be enough.

Marsden had had the sanction of the Church Missionary Society to remove John Butler and his son if he saw fit. If he could not shift Kendall, then Butler must go. The hand of God was seen to be behind the wreck of the *Brampton*. Matters came to a head when John Butler was said to have been drunk on board a ship in the Bay. A committee of missionaries found him guilty of 'inebriety' and this served as the means of his removal, a heavy charge, possibly justified, of which he would nevertheless be cleared by the Society when he finally returned to England. Butler, miserable and angry at his brethren's treatment, was forced to leave the mission and with his family and Marsden sailed for New South Wales on 13 November 1823. Kemp wrote that he had some feeling about his leaving 'having been together for some years past: but I am sorrow [sic] to say it was not, with that affection which as christians we ought to feel.'

Chapter 7

New Missionaries
1824

James Kemp, William Puckey Snr, James Shepherd and their families and William Spickman remained at Kerikeri, uneasily expecting Hongi to bring Kendall up to live with him on his land near the Wairoa Stream, or even into the Mission House. Hongi was in a cleft stick. He wished to bring Kendall to Kerikeri out of loyalty to his old friend, but did not want the other missionaries to go, as they had said they would, should Hongi carry out his intention. It is doubtful whether Kendall really wanted to be at Kerikeri unless he were reinstated in the mission. Certainly Kendall's family did not.

Henry Williams, James Kemp and Shepherd reasoned with Hongi. He could not put Kendall into the Mission House as Kendall would be punished if that happened for it belonged to the Society. They were already getting timber to build Hongi a house on Kororipo Point which Puckey could begin immediately. And furthermore the Rev. Samuel Marsden had appointed Kerikeri to be the place for a school which would benefit Hongi's children. Whether any of this swayed Hongi is dubious, but whatever his reasons he did not bring Kendall to Kerikeri. Two weeks later Hongi's house was begun by William Puckey and his son, fulfilling Marsden's promise to Hongi back in 1819.

The tapu on the river imposed in 1821 had at last been lifted with the removal of the remains of Tete and Apu from Kororipo Point to their final resting place inland, enabling the settlers to canoe the timber which had been destined for Sam Butler's house up from Te Tii without penalty. This would form the frame of Hongi's house.

The settlement was a hive of activity with the chapel and Hongi's European house being built. The wheat crop had to be got in. Although thin, it was declared 'plump and good' and stored in Butler's large barn.

Two of the three horses carried down by the *Dromedary* were at last brought in, saddled and ridden (the bones of the other were found). The new stockyard across the Kerikeri River now confined the milk cows, ensuring a supply of milk in season. The whole aspect of the settlement was one of promise and the settlers looked forward to being joined in a few months by George Clarke and his wife and child.

George Clarke's arrival had been eagerly anticipated by Hongi, as he was a gunsmith by trade, but Clarke was to come as a schoolmaster replacing Francis Hall. Hongi had been away at Kaipara in early 1824 and having made peace there, returned to Waimate just before Clarke and his family arrived at the Bay of Islands with the Duperrey Expedition on the French Ship *Coquille* from New South Wales. The Clarkes were joyfully received at Kerikeri on 5 April 1824. A few days later some members of the French expedition paid a visit, with junior officer de Blosseville recording that:

> *Round a pretty basin . . . stand the houses of the missionaries . . . There are six, made of wood and whitewashed; the Minister's is larger and more elegant than the others. They are all surrounded by a wall eight feet high of strong planks, the gates of which, continuously shut by strong locks, reveal the watchfulness of thieves and the curious . . . On a hill which overlooks the settlement Shongi's hippah is built; it comprises some sixty huts and its position did not strike us as very strong.*

It was not of course a fortified pa but a collection of whare, not by any means all belonging to Hongi. With the French expedition came an invitation from Marsden to Hongi to visit New South Wales, but Hongi would not accept, saying he feared he might be hung should he go there.

Clarke's presence did nothing to alter the behaviour of the New Zealanders towards the mission. In fact his earnest efforts to start schools and his refusal to mend their guns served only to arouse their contempt. The tribe began to steal again. Rewa and Wharerahi were indifferent to the missionary complaints, and haughtily replied 'We did not come in the night', Rewa adding that he now plundered the settlers because they did not make him presents as Butler had done. There were, he said, five or six chiefs at Kerikeri equal in rank, who had previously received unequal treatment. One of those aggrieved was Moka, Rewa's brother, a little man, beautifully tattooed, but an angry man, always troublesome. The missionaries rejoiced when Moka was at his place inland.

The New Zealanders still followed their centuries old ways, unmoved by the proselytising missionary. It was as Hongi had said. They were not ready to exchange their atua for the God of the missionaries. The white man had one forefather, the New Zealanders another. Their own departed spirits came back to speak to the living. An example of this was seen when a sick chief Wairua was brought in June to a hill across the Kerikeri River where he lay under a temporary raupo shelter attended by a number of slaves. By his side lay a tohunga. On the Sabbath the concerned missionaries went to find what they might do to help him, climbing up the 'common' path through the tapu land around the chief, by which the slaves brought his food. Hongi and the other chiefs were very angry. If the missionaries did not pay heed to their pollution of the tapu river, Tangaroa (God of the Waters) would cause a taniwha to upset their canoe. Paying no heed, the missionaries again crossed the river to see Wairua. Kemp offered to shake Wairua's hand, but Wairua refused saying his arm had been useless since he had shaken hands with him the previous Sunday. And, they were told, the tohunga and Wairua would have to move elsewhere if the large bell, which served as the settlement clock, was not silenced. Its constant noisy ringing would drive away the atua which was being invoked to cure Wairua. As would the noise of Puckey's hammering as he and his son worked across the basin on Hongi's European house.

Work on Hongi's house ceased for only a week, the chief recovered, and by the end of July 1824 it was finished. Thirty feet by twelve feet, timber lined, complete with fireplace probably of stone, and whitewashed, it stood on the ridge between the Kerikeri Basin and the Wairoa Stream. Puckey and his son then went to Paihia to work on the mission ship *Herald*, then being built. Wheat had again been sown in May of 1824. No bullocks had been broken in, but the horses were brought from across the river and harnessed to the plough. Kemp recorded

> *. . . it is the first time the horse has been worked the natives were much supprised [sic] to see the horse at work. I think they are likely to be very useful creatures in this land . . .*

Although wheat was again sown in the following three years, the return for the effort was poor. The farmer Davis, when he arrived later in 1824, declared the land poor and exhausted. Even earlier in the year there had been less wheat from the December–January harvest and all supplies were short. There was not enough food to maintain the native schools, let alone succour the New Zealanders who were in distress at having only fern root to eat. The constantly departing taua had severely depleted food supplies; as did the feasts which were given to the visiting Waikato people with whom Rewa was treating, and to the Kaipara people with whom Hongi was suing for peace. Any surplus potatoes and pigs were still being bartered with the shipping for guns and gunpowder. The slaves came off worst. When one of Shepherd's lambs was killed, Hongi beat three of his slaves for this act. Clarke, with little charity, wrote 'may it have a happy effect upon their minds'. Clarke's feelings are perhaps understandable as the depredations of the native dogs had greatly reduced their small breeding flock.

James Shepherd was still the butt of the new Zealanders' ire. Once, during a tug of war over a ram which Moka was trying to take, Shepherd was struck with a piece of wood. On another occasion Mrs Shepherd was also hit and spat at in the face several times. The Kerikeri tribes still considered that Shepherd did not belong to them but to Te Morenga. Shepherd at this time frequently travelled from Kerikeri to a hut built for him on Te Morenga's land near Pukenui.

The promised farmer, Richard Davis and his family, arrived at last in August 1824. With them came Charles Davis (no relation) a schoolmaster. Richard Davis immediately explored the possibilities of developing more suitable land for a farm at either Kahikatearoa, Parengaroa, Waimate or Pukenui (Te Ahuahu). Land at Pukenui near Lake Omapere belonging to Te Morenga's tribe was chosen. Here was good volcanic soil and plenty of timber and water. Within a short distance a thousand New Zealanders were said to live. But then Hongi Hika intervened. This was his old enemy's land. The only possible route to the Pukenui was through Hongi's territory, and this passage he would not allow. There the matter rested for a time.

The settlers turned to building a wharf (near to the present wharf) making carts for the supplies, and repairing rotting buildings and fences. The chapel built in 1823–24 was still unfenced, and around it, between the Mission House garden fence and the front-yard fences of the storehouse and Kemps' house, grazed the few goats and sheep which the New Zealanders had not killed or stolen. The story of the building of this first chapel at Kerikeri and of the chapel which succeeded it, to the time a church was built in the 1870s, is told in Section 2 of Part II.

Chapter 8

Years of Expansion
1824–1827

The bid to establish a farm inland was revived in October 1824 when Rewa proposed that the mission should farm some of his tribe's (Ngai Tawake) land at Waimate. Hongi countered with an offer of some land which he owned at Taiamai. Perhaps, the missionaries thought, Shepherd should go to Te Morenga's at Pukenui and the two Davises to Hongi's land. This might promote unity among the chiefs. But the tribal jealousies could not be so easily resolved and there were more skirmishes between Te Morenga's people and Hongi's, as there had been in 1819.

The attacks against Shepherd continued, one with a knife which could have been serious had Shepherd resisted. A meeting with the chiefs was arranged, as Moka's behaviour was largely at the root of the trouble, and now his actions were explained to the missionaries. He had been insulted on board ships, had a grievance over an insult to a chief by Puckey at Paihia, and Mrs Shepherd had struck his hand — the grossest insult. Moka's behaviour in Hongi's eyes was justified, and he too was indifferent whether Richard Davis farmed or not. Rewa, however, was upset at his brother Moka's behaviour. If the missionaries went away, he was heard to say, 'the Native Men may sit and look at each other when they want anything . . .'

So Richard Davis stayed for the time being, but it was agreed that Shepherd be removed for a time. He needed in any event to go the the colony (Sydney) to have 'a speck', which was growing across his eye, removed. Shepherd left on 15 December 1824 and Kemp wrote that he felt the separation very much. During this time fighting expeditions were in preparation to go against the Kaipara people to avenge the battle of Moremonui when Hongi's sister had been cruelly killed. The Kaipara tribes, however, came on a visit and on their departure Charles Hongi went back with them as a 'hostage of peace'. Parties of New Zealanders still came through the settlement from Hokianga to take their pigs to the shipping, that fruitful source of muskets, despite the constant insults they were offered by the seamen.

An incident with Hongi showed the impotence of the missionaries to interfere between Hongi and a musket. At dinner time at the Kemps' house one day

> *Shunghee came in, in his usual civil quiet manner, and sat down and partook of some dinner also. At the same time there was a run away Sailor sitting upon one of the logs of timber outside the fence; he had come up from the Harbour and had offered Shunghee a Musket for a girl out of one of the Missionaries' houses, unknown to us. Immediately after Shunghee rose from dinner, he went to Mr Clarke's house and called out a fine girl that had been a long time a Servant at Mr Kemp's and had been well taught, and was civilised and dressed in English clothing . . . Shunghee immediately hurried her into the Canoe that was waiting, and he and the fellow went off with her . . .*

The missionaries, afraid of arousing Hongi's anger and knowing they would have no success, did not attempt to follow them.

The summer of 1825 was again very hot. Te Morenga's tribe and Hongi's were still skirmishing inland. In early 1825 Davis, with the impasse over the land at Pukenui, went to join Williams and Fairburn at Paihia, with the thought that he might now farm at Kawakawa. The bogy of Thomas Kendall and rumours once more that Hongi would bring him to Kerikeri to live with him on the Wairoa, alarmed the Kemps and the Clarkes. The latest scare was short-lived, for Kendall and his family quietly left for Valparaiso in March where Kendall acted as a clergyman to the British Consulate for two years before returning to settle in New South Wales.

The Hokianga tribes had come to stay at Kerikeri in February preparing to fight the Whangaroa people to revenge the death of a chief's brother who had been killed in a battle with them thirty years before. Despite 'dancing and shouting in all directions' they 'behaved well' and left in company with some warriors from Waimate. In a short time they were back with spoils from the fight at Whangaroa, and some of the Hokianga people who had come down from Waimate after the planting of the winter potato crop, joined Hongi who was now preparing canoes to fight the Kaipara people. The attempts at making peace had come to nothing. 'This evening' wrote Clarke 'we have had a great display of the Military order of the Natives. They were reviewed with great pleasure by Shunghee scarce a man was to be seen but had a musket'. The chapel could not be used as the Hokianga people were camped all about the mission houses.

Clarke's school, begun in 1824, had not succeeded as the mission was continually short of food. Richard Davis lamented in a letter to a friend 'Mr Marsden is so very neglectful in supplying the mission.' The crops had been poor and the missionaries were forced to buy flour, so bad it could scarcely be eaten, from the shipping — a scandal in Henry Williams' view. George Clarke summed the situation up when he wrote 'have this day been one year in New Zealand, it has fast passed away, and very little has been done.' Planting wheat again at Kerikeri in May, Kemp fenced around the wheat fields for the first time, where so much had been destroyed by roaming animals in the past.

In May 1825 came the sad news of Charles Hongi's death at Kaipara and with it word that Hongi intended to stay there until the Kaipara people were destroyed. Some of the warriors were returning, much reduced by privations. Moka and Wharepoaka had both been wounded. In July Hongi too came back to Waimate. He told the missionaries he would be going to Whangaroa to enquire into the taking of the brig *Macquarie* by a tribe there the previous March, and punish them if necessary. 'I did little to dissuade him from going' wrote Kemp 'as they deserve to be punished.' Leaving from Kerikeri, Hongi 'manifested all the vivacity of a young man . . . never so lively as when about going out on a fighting Expedition.' However Hongi returned without fighting, bringing with him the brig's boat which he had taken from the tribe there, desiring it to be returned to New South Wales, proof to the missionaries of his good intentions toward them.

Revenge for his son's death at Kaipara now filled Hongi's mind — 'his life seems bound up in that of his sons.' Kemp tried to dissuade Hongi but Hongi replied that 'N Z man was very fond of fighting and he did not think that he would leave it off.' But, asked Kemp, had not his son died as a result? Hongi was deeply hurt by this remark. When, in December 1825, Hongi was taking farewell of the missionaries before going to fight again at Kaipara, Charlie's red jacket was returned to him by the missionaries, whereupon Hongi broke down and wept. Moved, Clarke wrote to the Church Missionary Society

> *. . . may the Lord preserve him from mischief and keep him from doing any, I do feel a strong affection for him for his kindness to us. I have never seen a Native as friendly to Europeans as gentle in his manners nor so affectionate to Europeans his good natural sense is also well known to you.*

Yet Hongi remained true to his ancestors and their ways until the day he died. Christianity would not touch him.

After Hongi, Rewa, Ururoa, Titore, Pakira and the warriors had gone, those left were near starvation and in early 1826 disease struck both New

The launching of the Herald *at Paihia in January 1826. A painting by M.R. Williams.*
AUCKLAND INSTITUTE AND MUSEUM

Zealanders and settlers. Mumps (the stockman Spickman was the only adult to have this) and influenza were rife. The mission itself had not received flour, salt or soap for months and the wheat had the blight. There were, however, some brighter patches for the missionaries. The most important had been the launching of the mission ship *Herald* at Paihia in January. This enabled the missionaries to go to New South Wales for goods, or to trade further afield than the Bay of Islands for food. At Kerikeri the schoolhouse/chapel had been fenced and the wharf finished and a boathouse was being built. The school staggered on.

But new missionaries were on their way — the Rev. William Williams, brother of the Rev. Henry Williams and his wife, and the lay settler James Hamlin, a flax dresser and weaver, and his wife. Marsden had planned for them to go to Parengaroa where Shepherd had been going to go in 1823, but early in 1826 William joined his brother Henry and his family at Paihia, while James Hamlin came to Kerikeri moving into the Mission House with the Clarkes. Puckey Snr and his wife had both been dismissed from the mission employ by this time for continued drunkenness, but their good and useful son William remained at Paihia with the Williams. The old raupo out-buildings near Puckey's quarters in the store were cleared away and the decayed kitchen outhouse demolished.

Hongi and Rewa and the fighting men were returning triumphant from another battle at Kaipara. Almost immediately Rewa began getting up a fight against the Paroa people on the south coast of the Bay of Islands in retribution for the slaying of his mother at Okuratope (a pa at Waimate) by these tribes some thirty years before. The Paroa people were given an ultimatum — come to Waimate or be destroyed. Hongi disapproved, but Rewa was not to be gainsaid. To Rewa now, muskets and powder were the principal things. He could with these wreak vengeance and increase his mana. By taking land at Paroa he would also be closer to the shipping for trade. The Paroa people left their land, some going to Whangaroa, some to Waitangi (where they were killed) and some to the Hokianga. Hongi took a remnant under his wing.

The important chief Wairua, who had been ill across the Kerikeri River in 1824, died early in 1826 at Oruru (Doubtless Bay) and his body was brought to the point at Kerikeri. Kororipo Point was, over the years, the scene of many tangihanga when chiefly remains were wept over before being taken inland to their last resting place. It was Hongi, William Williams wrote, who cleaned

> *the bones of his departed friend [Wairua], an office always performed by some great person if it is the body of a Chief and being greatly tabooed and in a most squalid garment; he appears a truly wretched object.*

Survivors from the former battlegrounds of Waikato and the Thames came in July to seek Hongi's protection, having been hunted 'like partridge upon the mountains'. Hongi allowed 200 of them to go to the Hokianga, but was upset to learn that one of their number, a nine-year-old boy, had been killed by the Kerikeri people and his flesh offered to Kemp. Rewa, after much discussion, set off for the Waikato with one of the Waikato chiefs to make peace, while Hongi announced his intention of making peace with the Thames tribe. A temporary peace reigned once more at Kerikeri.

In the mission settlement Hamlin, his wife and infant son James had moved from the Mission House into Puckey's old quarters in the store. Clarke had been with Henry Williams of Paihia in the *Herald* to Tauranga taking cuttings of peach and quince, pumpkin and other seeds from Kerikeri and they had successfully traded store goods there for a hold full of potatoes. The missionaries for the first time began to make regular visits to Waimate and places down the Kerikeri Inlet. But by September

1826 they were again short of provisions for the schools and workmen. Plans for new mission stations had to be postponed once more.

Hongi also now became cast-down and sullen. His daughter had died and a wife had eloped with his son-in-law. She then hanged herself, while his son-in-law attempted to shoot himself. Hongi tried to kill himself more than once, but was restrained by others of his tribe. The mission was alarmed on hearing the rumour that Hongi proposed bringing the people of the first New Zealand Company, then at Hokianga, to Kerikeri and oust the missionaries. The New Zealanders reasoned that their children died at the mission schools and that the Christian beliefs did not in any event exempt men from death. Besides, the missionaries were opposed to war and 'all men's customs' and the New Zealand Company was prepared to trade in fire-arms. This fortunately came to nothing, but the missionaries were shortly to share in Hongi's misfortunes and consequent loss of mana. In December 1826, a 'muru' of 200 from Waimate passed through, telling the missionaries that Hongi was 'broken' and the settlers would now be taken as slaves. Fences and outhouses were broken down for the nails in the boards, and goats were taken. Hongi's people retaliated by breaking four of their canoes.

Hongi became determined to remove to Whangaroa where there was a Ngati Pou pa which he said had once belonged to some part of his family and which Ngati Pou had refused to give up. The missionaries believed that this was only an excuse. Should he succeed in his intention, the shipping might be encouraged to put in at Whangaroa again for the easily accessible timber available and Hongi would benefit from the trade. Hongi left Kerikeri in December 1826 to pursue his goal. His wooden house on Kororipo Point, little used, was boarded up. Despite requests by the missionaries he would not sell it to them.

At the beginning of March 1827 James Stack of the Wesleyan mission at Whangaroa brought the distressing news of the battle there and of the possible sacking of the Wesleyan settlement. Clarke and Stack at once set out on the road to Whangaroa and met the shocked Wesleyan party already some six miles from their destroyed station. They were helped to Kerikeri and immediately sent by boat to Paihia. The news came of Hongi's possibly fatal wounding near Hokianga, and in the middle of the night the pregnant Mrs Clarke and the children were taken to Paihia. If Hongi were to die, the station was in danger, so great now was the emnity against him. Rewa and Moka passed through and warned of likely plundering, but could offer no protection. There were rumours also that Rewa would take possession of Paihia, where he was said to have a claim.

The whole mission made plans to evacuate Kerikeri. Goods were sent to Paihia and with other articles from that station were put on board a ship at the Bay. At Kerikeri Kemp wrote

> *in case Hongi should die and a plunder take place, most of the valuable property would be hid from the natives. We dug a very deep place in the Store . . . As Hatchets are implements of war we thought better to try to keep them out of their hands . . . for several months we knew not when we commenced cooking whether we should be permitted to eat or not or when we laid down to rest whether we should ever rise again . . . Our Boat was kept anchored stem and stern ready for flight . . .*

Rewa and Moka came again from the Wesleyan station with spoils taken from the tribe who had sacked it, including flesh and many heads which, while being cured near the mission houses, gave off such a 'disagreeable smell' that the doors and windows had to be kept closed. In the weeks which followed the missionaries carried on with their work. The chapel, derelict fences and the rotting store were repaired. James Hamlin began experimenting with New Zealand flax to test its suitability for spinning. Mrs Clarke after a few weeks at Paihia was able to return to Kerikeri.

Hongi at Whangaroa had been taken dressings and 'comforts' by the missionaries and although his breath whistled through the bullet hole in his chest, his continued existence even at a distance from Kerikeri stayed the hand of would-be plunderers of the missionaries. Nor was the mission molested this time when the chiefs Moka, Rewa, Wharerahi and Nene set out in their repaired canoes for a friendly visit to the Waikato tribes.

Marsden arrived again in March 1827 for a short visit of five days. Plans were made at this time for the two Mrs Williams to educate the mission's European girl children at Paihia, and a decision was taken to found a European boys' school at Kerikeri in the future. The New Zealanders were to be schooled with the European children as soon as the 'opportunity arose'.

By May 1827 the fear of Hongi's dying had abated and the goods buried in the store were dug up. On 9 May, Hongi 'cordial but thin and continually coughing' stayed at Kerikeri on his way to a hahunga at Waimate. There the chiefs quarrelled. Rewa informed the settlers that Hongi planned to take the missionaries back with him to Whangaroa. Rewa and a number of chiefs removed their canoes from the Wairoa lest Hongi should commandeer them when he came to Kerikeri, showing that although his mana was reduced he was still to be feared. Hongi, returning from Waimate with some hundreds of people, denied Rewa's report. It was true he had burned his whare at Waimate and would live there no more, but he would not burn his houses at Kerikeri in deference

to the feelings of the missionaries. On 5 June he left, and that day when Clarke went to check on Hongi's wooden house he found it, he wrote, 'the very picture of barbarism' besmeared inside and out with charcoal and red ochre. This was possibly a rahui — a sign to any New Zealander that it was not to be tampered with.

The mission, with Hongi gone, peaceful and more hopeful, went about its business. Trees were planted around the new fenced chapel. In August Kemp wrote 'We are endeavouring to form a Native Settlement at a short distance from us . . . One of them has erected a house where we intend the settlement to be.' This select native settlement was to be across the Waitotorongo Creek behind the mission houses. George Clarke reported with pride in the missionary committee minutes

> During the quarter the Natives have with some little assistance and instruction from me, erected a strong wooden bridge 60 feet long over a little river running on the southern side of the Settlement. A good road has also been cut upwards of 300 yds in length leading to and through the settlement.

The form of this 'road' can still be seen along the shore of the basin and

A sketch showing 'Kerikeri settlement, with a stage erected for a feast', reproduced from William Yate's An Account of New Zealand. *This engraving is a poor representation of the buildings at Kerikeri. On the hill next to the second chapel (1829) appears a two storey house. This was Charles Baker's lathe and plaster single storey*

continued on page 66

continued from page 65

home built in 1830. The two surviving original buildings are by the Waitotorongo Creek over which is the bridge designed by George Clarke and finished in April 1828. The hakari stage (a totally ridiculous shape) had been erected for a feast in February 1834. The building (exaggerated) in front of the incomplete Stone Store was likely to have been the cutting shelter of the stonemason Parrot.
AUCKLAND INSTITUTE AND MUSEUM

across the creek. The road and bridge were built in January 1828 to by-pass the existing path which went through the middle of the settlement between the store house area and the chapel to the New Zealanders' village on the hill. Rewa had given his permission for the road, but the Mangonui chief Tareha was furious at being denied his customary passage. 'No person can have any idea of his ferocity until they have seen him in a passion'.

Hongi made his last short visit to Kerikeri in November 1827 when most of the tribe from Waimate came to visit him there. He had by this time lost the use of his arm. He remained as kind to the settlers as ever, but his mana was waning in his decline. Rewa, however, was in the ascendant and the Ngai Tawake tribe from Waimate was spending more time cultivating at Paroa nearer to the Kororareka shipping. Rewa also prepared considerable quantities of flax for trade at this time. He and other chiefs suffered much humiliation at the hands of the seamen on the ships and Kemp expressed his fear that sometime the New Zealanders would have their revenge and the missionaries would suffer along with their compatriots.

At the mission settlement during late 1827 George Clarke and James Hamlin (who was proving to be an excellent linguist) continued to alternate between visiting small native settlements and taking the native school. Hamlin the flax weaver was also teaching some of the New Zealanders to spin in European fashion. Traditionally twine for flax clothing had been made by rolling the prepared flax strands rapidly with the heel of the hand upon the thigh.

The small mission ship *Herald* was now able to anchor within four to five miles of the Kerikeri Station, and it was a great relief not to have the heavy haul of goods by boat or canoe from Paihia. An iron crane had been made and erected on the wharf to land such goods, and the boathouse begun the year before was almost finished. This was the state of the settlement when the Rev. William Yate came to Kerikeri.

Chapter 9

William Yate's Little Empire
1828–1831

In January 1828 the Kerikeri settlement had a shot in the arm with the arrival of the Rev. William Yate who boarded with the Clarkes. Henry Williams was to write of him some six months later 'he is a considerable comfort to the mission — nothing can exceed his kindness and attention on all occasions.' Kemp was now excused his blacksmithing duties to concentrate on his position as storekeeper and on the erection of the new houses needed. Hamlin had permission to build a house, the studs and flooring of his store 'apartment' being quite rotten. The boundaries of the gardens were extended and Yate fenced a garden and planted native trees where his lath and plaster house was to be built in the churchyard near the 1824 schoolhouse/chapel. To this house, when built, he hoped to bring his 'beloved and valued' sister from England to keep house for him. Timber for the planned houses was to be bought from the European sawyers at the Hokianga Harbour, the Bay Maori being unwilling to trade their timber or labour for blankets which were the main mission currency by this time. The New Zealanders were well aware of the quality of different blankets and Kemp had to press the Society to send out thick large ones as those previously received for trade were of poor quality and eaten by moths.

Another wooden 'native' house was built across the Waitotorongo Creek in the Maori style and Yate hoped that this would tempt the natives to come and live with them. 'When the row is finished' he wrote,

> *it will have a very novel appearance from the River nay it will be magnificent for New Zealand, although there is not a window and only a doorway without a door.*

William Yate went out to the Maori encampments on a horse or a donkey. This donkey was probably one of two sent to New Zealand by the Wesleyan, the Rev. Samuel Leigh, in 1822. One had been used to bring the pregnant Mrs Turner to Kerikeri from Whangaroa in 1825. Many teretere came now to visit Kerikeri and instead of canoes being prepared for war on the Wairoa they were being made ready for fishing expeditions.

The great Hongi Hika died in March 1828 at Pupuke, Whangaroa. The Wakanui had at last sunk. His passing caused only one minor incident of plundering at the mission. It was said that his deathbed words had been for his people to go immediately to war, but for them not to harm the white people. The missionary Clarke wrote his tribute: 'His constant attention to Europeans made him generally respected among them: nothing could ever provoke him to take the life of a European . . .' and warmly added that he was a 'kind and affectionate parent no man could love his children more.'

Rewa, now the main protecting chief of the Kerikeri Station, was said by Yate to be 'the very reverse of his late predecessor Houngi, and his conduct though not so refined and imposing as that great man's is certainly very pleasing.' Rewa was not often at Kerikeri, dividing his time between Waimate and Paroa, when he was not away from the Bay. Yate called him 'a man of peace', a comparative phrase. Nevertheless Rewa was taken to task by the missionaries for prostituting his daughter aboard a ship for a fowling piece.

Yate's enthusiasm was not dampened, even by the dramatic news that the *Herald*, which in May 1828 had gone to Hokianga for timber and food, had been wrecked there. Although a severe blow to the mission in general in acquiring food supplies, the wreck proved only a temporary setback to Yate's building plans at Kerikeri. Timber would now be got at Puketotara (a branch of the Kerikeri River) and the logs floated down to the station. Flour was now shipped to the New Zealand mission from New South Wales, and Kerikeri bought wheat from the Waimate tribes, who had grown it for several years past from seed supplied by the missionaries. This was ground in an old hand mill.

The nurseryman Charles Baker and his wife had come to join the Kerikeri settlers in June 1828 and had moved in with the Kemps. Yate had spoken glowingly of Mrs Baker while they were all still in New South Wales. 'I am very pleased with the conduct of Mrs Baker. I think she will be of essential benefit to the station . . .' His opinion of Charles Baker was qualified. He was thought 'too much the gentleman' and would need to alter his ways. Baker, however, was to prove a useful and practical brother in the mission.

It was hoped that Hongi's wooden house on Kororipo Point might be bought and shifted to the settlement for the Bakers, but in September

1828 it was burned to the ground. Yate, with his gift for dramatising events, wrote:

> ... At a little after three O clock this morning we were all roused by the appalling cry of fire — on getting up we found that the house built for Hongi was one complete blaze. The scene was very grand as the house was fixed upon a high point of land jutting into the river the reflection of the fire upon the water reminded of the Bay of Naples.

Tareha was blamed for the blaze which razed the house. Rewa was furious. His desire had been to install in it the trader Capt. Kent who wished to marry his second daughter. But Yate was glad it was down. He had tried to purchase it from Rewa. Now, he wrote, it could not become a 'reseptacle for sailors'.

The Bakers could stay with the Kemps no longer and Charles Baker began to build a temporary raupo house close by where the new chapel was to be. Kemp, with the old chapel gone, extended his front boundaries to meet those of Yate. It may have been in this year that the ancient pear tree said to be the oldest exotic tree in New Zealand, was planted either in Kemp's yard or in Yate's. (There were two trees here in 1873.) It was not planted in its present place by Marsden in 1819 as is commonly said. In August 1828 Henry Williams was able to say of Kerikeri

> the schools have nearly doubled, the laying out of the ground around the Settlement has been [done] with great judgment and taste, and the projected buildings will add much to its appearance . . . Mr Yate sits as their common father — he is the man we have wanted — a few more of like spirit and we should advance.

Henry Williams would have to taste the gall of these remarks in the light of later events.

Yate was becoming reasonably skilled in the Maori language but the Maori understanding of the Christian belief was still imperfect. Many thought they should be paid for 'sitting still' on Sunday. New translations of the scriptures into Maori were needed. Of the subtleties of the 'moudi' language, wrote William Williams,

> much remains to be understood. As to the sufficiency of the language to convey to people the full meaning of the Scriptures, there cannot be a doubt, except in those peculiar expressions which it is necessary to introduce into every language which has previously been used only by heathens.

Few Maori stayed near Kerikeri now, but many passed through, camping for a few days. 'The Kerikeri' wrote Yate 'is the grand-highway to the sea and great numbers are constantly passing through the station with

Following pages: This sketch, entitled 'The Church Missionary settlement at Kiddeekiddee, New Zealand', was published in the Missionary Register *in 1830. It was probably executed in 1828. There is some wishful thinking in the sketch. The house in the middle foreground, the Rev. William Yate's, was never finished. The framework was given to Charles Baker for a new house to replace his temporary raupo one (1828, shown here next to the chapel on the hill). Note the clock in the chapel gable. The Mission House, with George Clarke and William Yate in residence, has the outside kitchen (1821) behind it and to its right is the large barn (1822). Two of the original buildings are on the left, the Store, with its 'apartments', in which James Hamlin was living (far left) and next to it James Kemp's house (1820) and the smithy. The landing stage was made in 1824 and the boathouse built in 1827.*
AUCKLAND INSTITUTE AND MUSEUM

whom we have much intercourse.' The most populous areas inland were Waimate and Pukenui (Te Ahuahu). The missionaries could now do almost as they pleased, Yate noted, as far as these Maori were concerned, as long as they did not infringe their customs.

One of the customs which the missionaries now found carried a strong tapu was fishing. Attempts to reach Mrs Shepherd who was very ill at Rangihoua were frustrated at first, and then, in running the gauntlet of the irate chiefs who were mending nets there, Mrs Hamlin had her cloak and baby snatched from her (both were returned). Another time Hamlin was shot at near Waitangi, although he was passing some distance away by boat. Hamlin recorded:

> *The natives in making their nets, they make them in parts and when it is thus finished they appoint the time for joining the parts together, during which time the sea is prayed over, and several other ceremonies performed; so that if a canoe passes; the persons belonging to the net strip them, and sometimes serious consequences are the result, in fact no body will dare to venture a canoe across the tapued or sacred place, except a chief of greater note than themselves, then they accommodate him because they cannot oppose him . . . If also the Priest is a true man and his God is not angry with him it rains on the second morning after it is commenced and then again as soon as it is finished joining together; but if all is not exactly right as the priest should wish it, and if they should not happen to catch many fish the priest throws the whole blame on those who made the net he himself is not allowed to feed himself such is the sacredness of his office at the time of joining the net together.*

Nor could the chiefs who joined the parts of the immense seine nets together feed themselves. On one occasion the Hokianga chiefs at Waipapa allowed the missionaries to come near on the grounds that the missionaries' persons were also sacred.

Peace and progress may have been the watchwords of the missions up to the end of 1829, but the peace was temporarily shattered with the event of the so-called 'Girls War' at the beginning of the year 1830. The long-standing hostility between the tribes on opposite sides of the Bay of Islands surfaced with a quarrel between New Zealand girls aboard Capt. Brind's ship lying with seven others at Kororareka. The quarrel continued ashore. Weeks of tension between the tribes followed when old grievances were revived, which culminated in a bloody battle on Kororareka Beach when almost one hundred people were killed. The battle raged again the following day when the great chief Hengi (a relation of Hongi Hika's) was killed. Pomare put a tapu on the beach, firing the few wooden houses there, and retired to his pa at Otuihu. The incensed tribes began to gather from inland.

This potentially serious affray had not directly affected the Kerikeri settlement. The Ngai Tawake had suggested that the brethren should build a fort there, as was being done at Paihia. But George Clarke had been adamantly opposed to the idea, as he perceived that it might involve the mission in the tribal quarrel, although the scriptures, the Church Missionary Society had previously informed them, contained no objection to fort building.

Some of the brethren at Kerikeri may have wished they had built a fort there when 300 Maori from Tahuna near Lake Omapere pitched their tents on the other side of the river opposite the mission. They were on their way to avenge the death of Hengi. But Yate seemed untroubled when he wrote,

The time has been when we greatly dreaded such a number of the natives as formerly used to break down our fences — kill the goats and many other such depredations but there is a great external change in the general conduct of the whole of the inhabitants of the Bay of Islands towards us. The Settlement presented a curious appearance today . . . The bush natives were collected in parties of about twenty each some talking — some dancing — some singing and the smoke of their fires rising from the midst of each party. There were seen a number of slaves with loads of firewood — there a great man with his gun, and his child. There an old woman scolding away at a famous rate because the slaves would not listen to her directions. In one place may be seen a lot of little naked children playing their pranks one with another and endeavouring to imitate the savage example of their parents and friends. In another place some of the more aged were trying their strength in paddling a Canoe. Our domestic natives were differently employed. Some few were hard at work, regardless of all that was passing around them; others seated on the tops of houses; with a spear in one hand a book in the other, and a pipe in the mouth, sometimes smoking and at others gazing upon the passing scene. The European children were all in the gardens, and the missionaries themselves were at their respective posts, or going about amongst the various groups that we may learn what was their intention . . . As to having any communication of a religious nature with them at such times as these is utterly impossible . . . We must go to them for they will not listen when they come to us . . . when we meet them at their own places, they are cultivating, or building, or doing nothing . . ., and they will listen to all we have to say.

Marsden, on his sixth visit to New Zealand had arrived at the Bay the day after the battle, and had immediately rallied the missionaries who mediated between the warring factions. With a truce at last achieved, Marsden now disclosed his plans for the long deferred farming venture. This was to be at Waimate, although in farmer Davis' opinion the land was

The mission station at Te Puna in the Bay of Islands, a pencil, pen and ink sketch by Richard Taylor, executed about 1841. The station was shifted here from nearby Rangihoua in 1832.
ALEXANDER TURNBULL LIBRARY

little better there than at Kerikeri. However, the Ngai Tawake was willing to sell and it was felt by the Kerikeri brethren that their settlement would become the key to the inland station.

Clarke, Hamlin and Yate from Kerikeri were chosen to go to Waimate. Yate did not wish to leave his little empire at Kerikeri, but, justifying Marsden's description of him as a 'faithfull missionary', agreed to go. The Rev. Alfred Nesbit Brown was to come to the station at Kerikeri. Only one minister at each station was the rule, although there would still be the two Williams brothers at Paihia. Rangihoua had only the lay settlers King and Shepherd, the latter having gone there on his return from New South Wales in 1826. These two now wished to move from their decaying houses and poor land around to the other side of Rangihoua Pa to the better climate and land at Te Puna. This was to be a source of friction. Rangihoua, Henry Williams had written, was a 'constant lounge' for the various officers from the shipping and Kerikeri not much better. His remarks were made in defence of the Paihia Station, said by many to be unsuitable because of its exposure to the 'evils' which came with its close proximity to lawless Kororareka.

The practical Williams brothers thought that either Kerikeri or Rangihoua should be immediately given up. They were not in favour of the farm at Waimate which they thought was unlikely to succeed and was merely indulging Marsden's 'hobby' of farming. Even if in time it was to make the mission independent of supplies from New South Wales, the energy expended could have been put to more fruitful purpose in converting the heathen further afield. And Rangihoua they thought useless for any purpose. But here Marsden felt the obligation to those tribes who had been the protectors of the first mission of 1814. It would be an insult to them should their missionaries be taken away. The Society agreed and the mission had moved to Te Puna by 1832. No stations at all were given up, and Waimate went ahead. Not a vestige of any whare remained on the hill at Kerikeri in 1830 and Yate's row of native houses had not been built. Instead the land across the Waitotorongo Creek (except for Kororipo Point) was bought as a farm for any Maori who might settle in the mission.

William Yate went to New South Wales during the year and brought back with him a youth, James Smith, a printer's assistant. A small printing

Facsimile of page 1 of the Catechism in Maori. *A surviving example of the first printings executed in New Zealand on the indifferent printing press brought to Kerikeri early in August 1830. The Rev. William Yate, assisted by James Smith, a 'printer's devil' from Sydney, printed first some hymns and* this Catechism *in late August and early September.*
AUCKLAND PUBLIC LIBRARY

press, the first in New Zealand, arrived in August 1830 and together Yate and Smith began to print translations into Maori. First off the press was a hymn, followed by a six page catechism, the liturgy and some more hymns. This printing press, however, produced such poor results, that the brethren later agreed that Yate should take translations of the scriptures to New South Wales to be printed in Sydney. This was done in the first half of 1833, Yate seeing them through the press, but the printing abounded with errors. It was not until after William Colenso and a new printing press arrived in 1834 that satisfactory books and pamphlets were printed.

For all his preaching of Christian values to the Maori, Yate's attitude towards their customs varied from those of most of his colleagues. The brethren were not above condoning utu when they thought it justified, providing it was carried out against the offender and not others who had no part in the offence. But Yate went further. He accepted the custom of muru, except where life was at stake. The custom of sometimes killing a woman caught in adultery he thought should not be interfered with — 'as it is now, the fear of death presents an obstacle to the frequency of the crime'. And infanticide, he said, was performed with the greatest decency. As to bigamy, he sent a plea to the Society to suspend their judgement on the plurality of wives until they had all the arguments on each side laid before them. A careful reply came back from the Society in London. While there was nothing in the scriptures to be found against bigamy, Maori preachers should refrain from this practice.

Yate felt the need to go to London to see the Society for a variety of reasons having, he said, several matters of great importance to lay before them. Apart from the opinions outlined, he wanted to give them his and the Kerikeri/Waimate side of the unhappy differences that had developed between them and the Paihia community. And probably what mattered most to him personally, he went to quash the rumours which may have reached their ears through Capt. Brind, whom Yate had heard would charge him 'with crimes of a most gross and horrid nature'. He felt he should not be condemned unheard. Yate went to England in 1834 but in Sydney, on his return journey, he had to defend himself against allegations of intimacy with the third mate of the vessel he had returned on.

The New Zealand brethren, to rid themselves of contamination, held a fast day, burning Yate's belongings and shooting his horse at Waimate. James Kemp at Kerikeri, whose son had been put into Yate's care for the journey to England, wrote to his son commanding him to destroy any gifts of Yate. Chapman indicated later that he had had suspicions of Yate's homosexual tendencies when they shared the Mission House. Yate's sorrowful sister (still in England), loyal to her brother, wrote bitterly to the Society that the destruction of her brother's property was

A comparatively innocent action to that of shooting an unoffending horse which with great care my dear Brother had trained for my use that I might visit the Native females at their own residences . . . What will the christian world say when it is made acquainted with the heathenish spirit of those who are appointed to preach the Gospel to the New Zealanders. Can this conduct be justified by any law human or divine? Ought not the perpertrators of such a barbarous act if they chose to show an example of revenge to the heathen, by shooting a valuable horse, and burning a person's private property to be made to pay for it? . . .

The mission station at Waimate. George Clarke's house is on the right, Richard Davis' to the left and James Hamlin's centre. An engraving from the Missionary Register, 1847.
AUCKLAND INSTITUTE AND MUSEUM

Whether Yate's generosity in personal expediture on the mission and the loss of his possessions were compensated for, as his sister wished, is not known. The missionaries, as William Williams wrote, regarding Yate as having brought 'so much dishonour on the holy cause of Christ in this land', had turned their fearful piety against him. (The Rev. William Yate was finally dismissed from the Society's service in February 1837.)

To return to the situation at Kerikeri in 1831, it soon became clear that although the Williams brothers may not have won the battle to disband either Kerikeri or Rangihoua, they did succeed in keeping the Rev. A. N.

Brown at Paihia and establishing the Boys' School there. However, the proposal to build a Stone Store at Kerikeri was the last straw for Henry Williams who opposed it from the start. The mission during 1831–32 was, wrote Brown, buried in secular concerns. Furthermore mission expenses had been incurred in New South Wales in 'a dark and intricate manner'. This was an oblique reference to the way in which Yate, who had spent some time in New South Wales and had the support of Marsden, had ordered many goods on behalf of the New Zealand mission. Brown's remarks were not unjustified. Houses were being built at Te Puna and Waimate, and the road to Waimate with its large bridge had cost much in manpower and money. The Society said later that the New Zealand mission had cost more than any other. The followers of Yate amongst the brethren were also able to outvote the others at missionary committee meetings.

Those left at Kerikeri were still sore at not having the Boys' School there but had pressed ahead with improvements to the settlement which added to their comfort. Charles Baker had replaced his raupo house up by the new (1829) chapel with one built of lath and plaster, the timber of which had come from the dismantled frame of Yate's partly built house down by the basin. Kemp had built a stone walled kitchen onto his 1820 dwelling. The road to Waimate did not extend down the hill to the wharf, but there was a path running from here at an angle up to Baker's house and the Chapel. The land which had been Yate's garden was divided, with Kemp extending his boundaries to meet those of the Mission House where Chapman now lived, following Clarke's departure for Waimate in early 1831.

The everyday tasks of building, maintenance and cultivation took up most of the brethren's time, causing George Chapman to write to the Society begging for help to be sent and suggesting

> *a young man that would wear on a hiring day in his hat a tuft of wool and a knot of horsehair and if he could milk so much the better . . . a young man who would know nothing beyhond his bible duties, and the length of plough he would come out to handle.*

What they did get eventually was John Edmonds who arrived in 1834 to build the Stone Store. But by this time the stonemasonry was virtually completed. The building of the Store from its conception to its completion and the uses to which it was put up until the turn of the century are the subject of Section 3 of Part II.

Chapter 10

Decline of the Mission
1831–1837

In 1831, at about the time that the Stone Store plans were under way, the protecting Ngai Tawake tribe at Kerikeri were pressing the settlers to buy a large tract of land surrounding the Kerikeri Mission. This was the so-called Children's Land.

Representations had been made by the brethren to the Church Missionary Society in London regarding the education and future prospects of their children in these most distant and isolated islands. When they reached the age of fifteen years, support from the Society for missionaries' sons ceased, although unmarried daughters continued to receive a half allowance. There were two options open to sons in a country without government and where the minute European population was still concentrated in the Bay of Islands. They could either work for the mission or farm to support themselves.

Opportunities for mission employment were limited and the Society in 1830 had reluctantly acknowledged that it would be necessary for the missionaries to buy land, against the day when their children would no longer receive the Society's allowances. But, cautioned the Society, any such private purchases, while being sufficiently near a settlement to afford protection, should also be far enough removed so as not to inconvenience it. Any land, it was further decreed, was to remain in the family of an individual as long as there were legal heirs in New Zealand to succeed, but otherwise the land should revert to the Society which would decide whether it should be sold.

With this directive in hand, the Kerikeri missionaries purchased the 3000 acres offered by the Maori, to be held in trust until the time came to set apart portions for their numerous children to farm. Well over a decade later, in Governor Grey's time, the missionaries would have to defend themselves against accusations of land grabbing as a result of this and other private purchases.

Having, however, bought the land, the future of their children must have seemed as secure as it was possible to make it. But in October 1831 the rumour reached the mission that a French corvette was on its way to New Zealand with the design of taking possession of the country in the name of the French Government. Should this happen there would be no future for any of them in New Zealand. The alarmed Kerikeri missionaries immediately took action.

> *All the principle chiefs of the Bay of Islands met today at our Settlement to consider the propriety of requesting King William to make them his allies to prevent themselves from the yoke of any other foreign power*

wrote the excited Charles Baker. Probably stirred up by William Yate, thirteen chiefs, including Rewa, Titore and Patuone (Hokianga) signed the petition which was forwarded to England. Although their fears were groundless, a consequence of this scare, along with growing anxiety about the behaviour of the shipping and the increasing number of speculators from New South Wales who were buying up land at the Bay, was the appointment of a British Resident, James Busby, who came to New Zealand in 1833. A 'man o' war without guns' as he was to be termed, was not what the missionaries had hoped for. They had wanted a British navy ship which would patrol the Bay and the coast, protecting the Maori from exploitation by the shipping. The future of their children, too, was precarious without protection, but colonisation of any description they did not want.

In the meantime, Henry Williams, Superintendent of the Mission in New Zealand, had been turning his attention to peacemaking among the tribes to the southward and to exploring the possibilities of extending the mission there and to the north. He remarked that they, the missionaries, were now nearly as thick as grasshoppers at the Bay. Yate, as Secretary of the Church Missionary Society Committee in New Zealand, wrote asking the Parent Committee to suspend any southward move until it had the support of the New Zealand Committee. Months later came the advice — we haven't any funds to let you go southward. This probably suited the Waimate/Kerikeri settlers but frustrated Henry Williams, who saw all the money being spent on the white elephant store at Kerikeri and the unprofitable farm at Waimate. In his anger, he refused to allow all the goods coming from New South Wales to be landed at Paihia, as was usual. Each settlement, he informed the other stations, would have to make its own arrangements.

'Peace and Harmony' was at last restored between the settlements in

1834. Approval had come from the Society in London to extend the missions to the southward, cheering the heart of the 'angry brother' Henry Williams. However, the missionaries were exhorted to look to the Maori to extend the missions. They, the Society thought, would be more effective than Europeans, in their use of the Maori language, in their knowledge of customs and in their mode of thinking. A not small consideration was that they could also be employed more cheaply! The Society was still short of funds. Carrying of the Christian message far afield by the Maori was, in fact, happening spontaneously and many tribes too, were asking for a missionary. Baker, who had been going with Matthews and Puckey to establish a mission at Kaitaia to the north, was forced by the illness of his wife to remain at Kerikeri. She was convinced she was dying and had got to the point of calling their child to her bedside to hear her final words. Storekeeper Thomas Chapman went to Paihia, and James Shepherd left his newly built house at Te Puna to become storekeeper, moving into Chapman's vacated house, the original Kemp home. He was assisted in storekeeping duties for a time by a new arrival, John Morgan, who was, before long, to start, with Preece, the first southward mission at Puriri on the Waihou River at Thames. Kemp was now in the Mission House.

With the arrival of John Edmonds and his large family in New Zealand in 1834, pressure was put on the Kerikeri Mission. The Kemps by this time had seven children, the Bakers six, and the Shepherds six. Now were added five more of the Edmonds. There was much resentment at

A pen and ink sketch of the Bambridge family returning to Waimate 22 July 1844, drawn by W. Bambridge in his journal. Bambridge recorded that they were at time "jolted over stones in some instances $1^1/_2$ foot high . . ." At the slippery Waimate bridge over the Waitangi River the oxen were taken over detached from the load. "I expected to see them tumble into the stream below" wrote Bambridge. George Clarke had designed both this bridge and the Kerikeri one of 1828. Clarke and Hamlin, assisted by Maori, constructed the road in 1830.
ALEXANDER TURNBULL LIBRARY

Decline of the Mission

The mission boat, the Karere *(Messenger), accompanying a New Zealand war expedition. The illustration comes from William Yate's* An Account of New Zealand.
AUCKLAND INSTITUTE AND MUSEUM

A pencil sketch by the Rev. Richard Taylor showing a 'n.w. view of Mr Shepherd's house, Wangaroa 13 Nov. 1841'. The chapel was built into the end of the dwelling
ALEXANDER TURNBULL LIBRARY

Edmonds' appointment by those who had 'born the burden of the heat of the day'. Although he was destined for Kerikeri, it was not until the Bakers moved to Paihia that he left Shepherd's Te Puna house and moved into the vacated Baker home up by the chapel.

Kemp and Shepherd were taking their proselytising on Sundays to the small Maori settlements within riding or boating distance. Maori were still passing through Kerikeri on their way to the Bay, staying for short periods. A request came from Hongi's son, who was living at Whangaroa, for a mission station to be established there. For a time Kemp and Shepherd argued over who should go, as only two people were now needed at the Kerikeri Station. Edmonds, it was thought, could stay to do the manual work, while whoever else stayed could look after the store and the flour which would be coming down from the farm and mill at Waimate. Both wrote to the Society. Kemp pleaded that his peculiar trials should merit him first consideration and spoke of Mrs Kemp's 'advanced' years. Shepherd wrote that his wife's condition was bordering on insanity, she having made thirteen moves in as many years. Neither would make the move, so both stayed put until 1839.

During the intervening years, Henry Williams was continually pressing for Kerikeri to be relinquished. But Kemp begged that the light might not of argument. The land was subdivided among the mission progeny and with the passing generations sold to others. The old understanding between Maori and missionary was forgotten.

Far from claiming the 13,000 acres originally purchased in 1819 (part of this had been rebought as the Childrens' Land) the Society asked for a grant of only 350 acres. The Land Commissioners allowed 345 acres which included all of the buildings on the basin at Kerikeri and the ridge, bought separately in 1831, where the Maori whare had been in the early years of settlement. The grant excluded Kororipo Point which Kemp had bought in 1838. Old James Kemp wrote to a friend in 1857

> *My Tribes have their farms of wheat, cattle, sheep etc and they have their little vessels to take their produce to the different Ports for Sale, they have also water mills to grind their grain and drays with teams of horses . . . to plow . . .*

At that time, too, native preachers gathered the christianised Maori into the chapels built by the tribes in many villages. It seemed for a time, as if Marsden's dream for the Maori was becoming a reality. But the momentum of events was to overrun the missionary ideals. With continued immigration to New Zealand, and the large confiscations of Maori land following the Land Wars of the 1860s, much good land passed into Pakeha hands. With the land gone, the mana of a tribe was lost. With the

This engraving, titled originally 'Night scene in New Zealand', shows James Kemp preaching to Maori. It comes from the Missionary Register, 1837.
AUCKLAND INSTITUTE AND MUSEUM

law of tapu replaced by European law, the hereditary dignity of chiefly descent diminished. With the population depleted by introduced diseases, and ravaged by the effects of liquor, communities lost heart. Perhaps most importantly over the next century, the Maori language, in which was embedded the culture — the knowledge of their own history, skills, ancestry and observances — was subjugated. The language and the world of the Maori had been learned together. Parted, they could be lost and die.

Scattered cockle shells from the middens of generations, the softened contours of terraces and scarps are all that are to be seen on the old pa site on Kororipo Point. The tribes are gone from here, but the land remembers the ancient ways.

Part II

Section 1
The Mission House

Section 2
Chapel, Schoolhouse and Church

Section 3
The Stone Store and Mill

Section 4
The Waterfalls

The old pear tree growing on Kemp's property at Kerikeri in October 1949. The outbuilding, known as the old blacksmith's shop, was erected in 1832. It was where James Kemp made the iron work and Ben Nisbet did his carpentry for the Stone Store. The present curator's cottage is in the same position.
NATIONAL PUBLICITY COLLECTION/ALEXANDER TURNBULL LIBRARY/
E. CHRISTENSEN PHOTOGRAPHER

Above: *New Zealand's earliest surviving buildings of wood, and of stone. On the left, the Stone Store (1831-36); on the right the Kemp House (1821-22). The later St James Church (1875) on the hill replaced an 1829 chapel.*

Left: *The view from Kororipo Pa across the Kerikeri Basin. The first bridge to cross the Kerikeri River was built in 1913.*

Above: *The dining room at Kemp House, looking through the hall to the front door.*

Left: *The fireplace in the dining room. Opened, the cupboards reveal a servery to a pantry.*

Wisteria frames the verandah of Kemp House. The exterior and the original (1821-22) front rooms have been restored to ca. 1843 by the Historic Places Trust. The skilling dates from the Kemp's occupation in 1832. Upstairs, the bedrooms are much as they would have appeared in the late nineteenth century.

Right: *The sitting room at Kemp House.*

Above: *The back of Kemp House from St James Church grounds. At left is the curator's cottage built on the site of Kemp's 1832 smithy.*

Left: *One of a set of chairs brought by Francis Hall from England in 1819.*

The ground floor of the Stone Store is at present used as a local store and souvenir shop. Ephemera of historic interest have been collected and displayed by the lessee on the first floor.

Left: The date 1833 was engraved on the arch above the doors of the Stone Store when the builders 'struck centre'.

Above: *The Waianiwaniwa Falls.*
Right: *The Wharepoke Falls. Walking tracks to both falls begin near the Kerikeri Basin. The Waianiwaniwa Falls are easily reached by car, where there is a pleasant picnic area, with viewing platforms overhanging the 'Waters of the Rainbow'.*

ALL PHOTOS IN THE COLOUR SECTION: FRANK EASDALE

Part II

Section 1

The Mission House

The Rev. John Butler, on 10 October 1821, wrote a despondent letter to the Church Missionary Society setting out the difficulties experienced by the missionaries since settling at Kerikeri, and in particular by himself and his wife. When he was in a dwelling of his own, instead of the wretched hovel he had lived in for nearly two years, he would be able to learn the language and preach therein to the New Zealanders. And Mrs Butler was rendered wretched by having to slave in an outdoor kitchen shed which was the slaughterhouse for the settlement 'while other women were sitting at home in comfortable houses with little to do . . .' This was an oblique reference to Mrs Kemp and the Hall/Kemp house built the previous year.

With this letter and his diary to the end of September, he sent to the Society in London a ground plan of his garden and house layout. Butler's diaries at this period are full of his efforts to get a house for himself. There is no doubt he needed one, for the quarters in the storehouse in which he, his wife and young daughter Hannah lived were cramped and primitive. William Hall of Rangihoua, who oversaw the erection of buildings, and the mechanics who built them, thought Butler's plans too grandiose and expensive. Hall described the house Butler required.

Mr Butler wants a house built 40 feet long, 16 feet wide and 20 feet high with a viranda at the back part of it, suported with colums and enclosed with palisading, and a room of 8 feet square under each end of the Viranda the house is to be two stories high with a Hall and a staircase in the centre of the building, a circular fanlight and pilasters at the Front door the doors are all to be six panneled work on both sides with double faced Architraves double hung sashes and framed Shutters — and every other part corresponding. Mr Butler complains he has been nearly 18 months at New Zealand and never got a house yet, but it is more than probable that it will be more than 18 months longer before the house is finished that he wishes to have, as above described.

Hall also commented that getting the timber from the Waikare, which the natives at that time would anyway only sell for muskets and powder, would have to be towed between twenty and thirty miles.

William Hall wrote this letter shortly after Marsden who had been in New Zealand from February to December 1820 had returned to New South Wales. He had talked over Butler's plans with Marsden, who, being uncertain whether Butler would start a settlement in the Waitemata Harbour or stay at Kerikeri, told Hall that he would agree to the house proposal 'provided Mr Butler stays at New Zealand, but if he go away, Mr Marsden has directed me to build a plain house.' The carpenters employed by the mission, Bean and Fairburn, were let the contract for £250 — 'for the workmanship only, all materials to be prepared ready to their hands'. William Hall thought that Bean's and Fairburn's estimate compared well with New South Wales prices.

The site for the house was probably settled at the time the mission was established at the end of 1819. While Francis Hall's and the Kemp's house was being built in early 1820, John Butler laid out and fenced the garden area which was to surround his home. By the end of May 1820 a paling fence enclosed the area shown on the plan and several 'esculents', that is edible plants, had been sown including cabbages, broccoli, onions, shallots, pumpkins, carrots, turnips, radishes, lettuce, endive, asparagus, celery, melons, cresses as well as beds of hops propagated from one root brought from Port Jackson.

In July 1820 the three-year-old son of the Beans died and was buried near to the back fence of Butler's garden, there being no churchyard site set out then. The burial site is marked upon the plan as a 'Burial Ground'. John Butler wrote feelingly of the occasion,

> *This afternoon I buried Mr Bean's child in my garden. All the Europeans attended and walked in regular succession as this tender lamb was the first Xian that it has pleased our heavenly father to take to himself & shelter in his bosom from our little flock of Kidie Kidie.*

By August of 1820 Butler was beginning to wish that Hall's and Kemp's house was finished. Bean and Fairburn had been working on it since January, and until it was finished they could not take up their contract for Butler's house. Timber still had to be got and prepared for them, and William Hall who had been helping Marsden get a cargo-load of spars for the *Dromedary* could not help with procuring timber for Kerikeri.

At last, in September 1820, two fine logs were obtained. With these

The Mission House

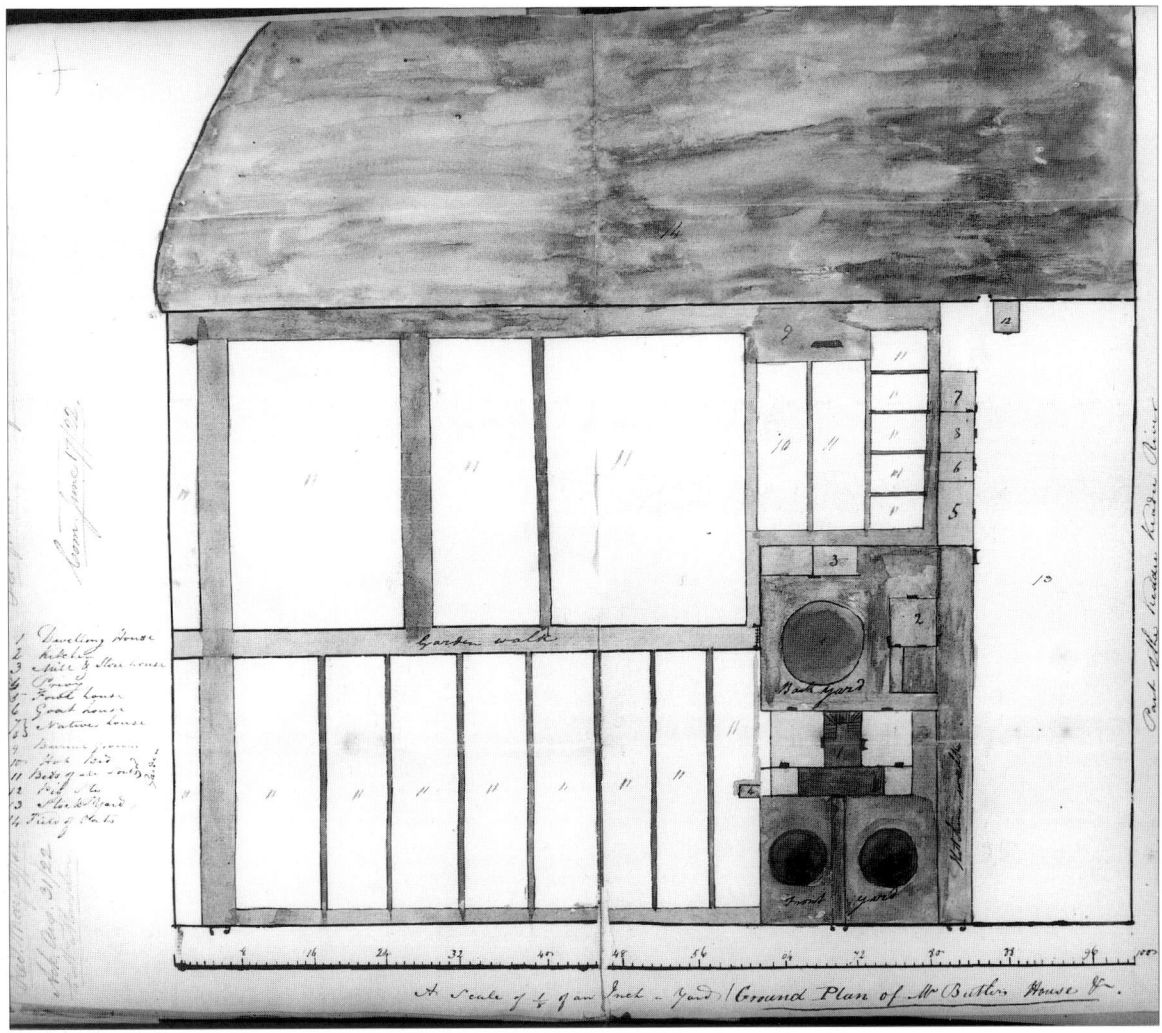

Ground plan of the Rev. John Butler's house at Kerikeri, sent to London with a copy of Butler's Journal early in 1821. The house frame was not put up until August 1821.
HOCKEN LIBRARY, DUNEDIN

Key

1. Dwelling House
2. Kitchen
3. Mill and storehouse
4. Privy
5. Fowl house
6. Goat House
7. Native's house
8. Native's house
9. Burial ground*
10. Hop bed
11. Beds of all sorts
12. Pig sty
13. Stock yards
14. Field of oats

* The burial ground was where the three-year-old son of William Bean, the carpenter, was buried in 1820, the year in which Butler's garden was laid out and planted. All later burials were on the hill near the present church.

prepared, an outhouse kitchen twenty-eight feet by sixteen had been put up by the beginning of December. This building was termed 'the old American house' in another despairing journal entry of Butler's a few weeks later.

> *I am truly sorry to see the building department go on so slow. The Carpenters are very dilatory and shamefully negligent. The native Sawyers are become very idle: first, because they are not now as formerly paid in muskets & powder: secondly, because they are very badly looked after . . .*

He had had, he said, to be ploughman, vine dresser, storekeeper. He had gone to the pit to dig clay, to the wood to fell trees and tugged at the oar night and day. William Hall had not exerted himself to get timber and he had been obliged to turn carpenter himself while others appointed to manual labour grew careless and negligent. Now, he had engaged native sawyers to go to the Kahikatearoa Wood to cut timber 'for outhouses and fence in a spot even if I never get a house erected upon it'. He and his family 'were virtually living out of doors and not a single foot of timber at present toward a house for me to live in'.

Butler also wrote to Marsden in New South Wales complaining of William Hall's unhelpfulness and of there being no timber at Kerikeri, 'and the old American house stands as you left it, save there are a few shingles on one side.' In fact, at this time, in early 1821, Bean and Fairburn were going on with the shingling of the kitchen outhouse, and the criticism of William Hall was harsh as Hall's wife Dinah had just had a baby which kept him at her side.

When Butler had relinquished his position as Superintendent of the mission the previous year, complaining that he could not control the mechanics or labourers, Marsden had said 'If you cannot manage the carpenters I am sure I cannot'. Of this remark Butler had written defensively 'they ought to be sent back, and not remain here to eat the bread of idleness, and dip their unhallowed fingers in the purse of charity'. Butler had antagonised the employees of the mission from the beginning with his unfortunate personality. Unhappy and isolated, deprived of his former control as Superintendent, having a house seems to have obsessed him.

The end of January 1821 saw him a little more hopeful. Two huts had been built for the native sawyers beyond the Waianiwaniwa Falls near the Kahikatearoa Wood which the missionaries assumed they had bought with the payment for the land. Eight kauri were felled here, between seventy and ninety feet tall and four feet in diameter. The problem was how to get them down to Kerikeri. They had been going to make a track for bullocks to pull them out, but the cattle were not yet broken to yoke. The only thing to do was to wait for a flood when the logs could be floated down the Kerikeri River. In the meantime more trees could be felled and the river cleared of debris. Then came another setback. The native sawyers struck and felling ceased. Extra payment was being demanded for the forest by the chiefs. This was duly paid in mission goods.

A further boost to house building was given by the decision of the missionary committee in early February to supply William Hall with the necessary trade to barter for timber from the Waikare/Kawakawa natives, and to employ 'poor sailors' left by the shipping in the Bay. By the end of February fifty-four logs were got up to Kerikeri. William Hall had also sawn at Rangihoua 1218 feet of timber for Butler's house. While waiting, Butler put up a fence to enclose his house site within the garden enclosure, and in March induced the carpenters to help at Kahikatearoa, though Butler commented that they were proud and idle, would not sharpen a saw and offered him personal abuse.

Forty-two logs were waiting at Kahikatearoa for a flood by the middle of March. The logs from Waikare were being cut by eight native sawyers at the sawpits down near the Kerikeri Basin, about where the road now bends around the Stone Store. Twenty-four more logs were got from Waikare in April by William Hall, while Bean and Fairburn worked partly at Kahikatearoa and partly on shingling the kitchen outhouse. Butler had a row with Bean over the kitchen, pointing out what he thought to be right or wrong, but Bean would not obey him, saying he was under Francis Hall's general superintendence. He was, however, pleased with the native sawyers whom Mrs Butler cooked for, and with some of the timber they had cut he built a goat shed and an outhouse in his garden.

At last the rain came and with it the flood. Thirty-two logs were got over the Waianiwaniwa Falls, thirty logs reaching the settlement down the cleared river by 9 June. Butler's hopes of having a house by Christmas 1821 seemed possible when Bean and Fairburn took up their building contract on 11 June. A storehouse thirty feet by twenty had also been begun. Later it would be called a barn, the first at Kerikeri.

Despite the chief Tareha's taking away the native sawyers for a few days, Butler felt that the house would be finished in eight months' time. This second estimate proved to be just about right, despite the troubles which were to come. At the beginning of July Bean and Fairburn had the frame and the roof of the Mission House prepared, while Thomas Foster the blacksmith at Rangihoua had made twelve iron cramps and screwbolts to erect the skeleton. Puckey Snr was preparing timber for sheathing.

Then Hongi Hika returned. The sawyers struck once more and building stopped for a time. Butler had some solace in planting a great variety of seeds brought by the ship Hongi had arrived in. Ash seeds, acorns, hawthorn berries, hazelnuts, walnuts, cherry and plum stones, all went into his garden beds. A raspberry bed was made, and two acres of grass, trefoil and taru, were sown. With Francis Hall helping Butler to trim logs, the work on the house went forward and by August Bean and Fairburn had the frame of the main building and the verandah up.

Hongi's antipathy to Butler erupted later in August when a party of natives climbed over the seven foot paling fence, trod down his growing crop, ran over his garden beds and shot bullets at his garden seat. The prospect of further attacks caused Butler to suggest that work should stop on the house until the tribes had gone to war. The only thing to do in the circumstances seemed to be to finish off the kitchen outhouse. Puckey and Butler's son Samuel were aided by Boyle the saltman and John Lee the bullock man. Although the latter two were often drunk and beat the native sawyers, the kitchen was lined and limewashed and a chimney put up and plastered. At the end of September Butler was able to record:

> *I have moved my family into the kitchen; altho it is not finished, there being no window or upper floor at present. However, this is much more comfortable than the wretched place I lived in before.*

The kitchen/outhouse as shown on the plan is only a few feet away from the main house and appears to have consisted of two rooms with a chimney at the rear of the square room. A door led into the adjacent room which was possibly a pantry/storeroom, and another door from the kitchen gave on to what was probably a small verandah.

A week after removing to the temporary quarters in the kitchen, John Butler set off for New South Wales. The warriors had gone in September and Bean and Fairburn were able to get on with the house. Their contract was to finish at the end of March. Twenty-four more logs were got from the Waikare in December, enough to complete the work of sheathing.

The warriors had returned to Kerikeri in December 1821. Kororipo Pa with the waters around it had been made tapu and the missionaries had broken the tapu by towing the logs into the basin. The chief Wairua, of Cavalli Island, had threatened to break the house. An axe was given in utu for the offence, and Hongi's advice, when consulted, was to take no notice of anything Wairua might say. Nevertheless Bean and Fairburn went to Rangihoua, working there for a week until the affair had cooled.

John Butler returned in February 1822, and it is most likely that amongst the goods he had bought in Sydney were bricks for the Mission House chimneys. The bricks made at Kerikeri in early 1820 were not a great success and although these may have been used, perhaps re-used from the Butler's old storehouse/outhouse by the Waitotorongo Creek, many hundreds were needed for the tall chimneys of the Mission House.

With Butler's return, Bean and Fairburn left their quarters in the store

'Mr Kemp's House, Kerikeri', a sketch by Richard Taylor dated 9 August 1841. The skilling has been built on, 1832-34, but the original 1821-22 verandah with its two rooms remains.
ALEXANDER TURNBULL LIBRARY

and lodged with the Butlers in the outhouse kitchen for eighteen shillings a week. They built the two chimneys through March and early April and finished the interior details of the house, such as shelves in Butler's study, mantelpieces and window shutters for which Kemp had made holdfasts. They were paid ten shillings a day for the few extra weeks' work. John Butler was able to get the house and yard cleared of rubbish in time to hold a service in the new house on 18 March and a week later was moving in.

The account of Bean and Fairburn for the Mission House and 'other work', presumably not specified in the contract, amounted to £317.2.8, £67.2.8 more than the contract price of £250. Added to this would have been the cost of trade for timber, additional payment to Rewa for the Kahikatearoa Wood, 'wages' of the native sawyers, and the work of the blacksmiths, Foster and Kemp. All work was charged to the cost of buildings. Then there was the cost of the kitchen/outhouse. The Rev. Thomas Kendall's son from Rangihoua had also worked as an apprentice carpenter to Bean and Fairburn for some months, but as an apprentice would probably only have had his keep.

It must have been an expensive establishment in the end, but Butler was at last satisfied and was able to spend many hours in his study, well furnished by 1824 with maps and globes. His study was most likely to have been the small room opposite the top of the stairs, or just possibly the attic room. The house was not painted until September, by which time paling partly enclosed the verandah between the two small rooms which led off the two main downstairs rooms. The exterior paint was of white lead mixed with oil and turpentine. Lime made from burnt shell and mixed with white lead was used to whitewash the interior. A 'road' was made to the kitchen at the rear and it is possible slabs of wood were laid to surface the area between the kitchen and the back door of the house, as was done at Rangihoua.

With all in order in and about the house, Butler turned his attention to the building of a substantial barn. Fifty-four logs were rafted from Waikare in December 1822 and, as Butler wrote, 'By dint of very great exertion in exciting my natives and working with them almost beyond my strength in the heat of the sun, and by the continual assistance of the Lord . . . .', he was able to complete this forty foot by seventeen foot barn in time for the January 1823 harvest. Shepherd put his wheat into Butler's old barn (the storehouse on the Butler plan) which had thatched sides and a roof of raupo. Timber had been at a premium, and certainly roof shingles were a problem as no suitable timber had been found. Locally made shingles let the rain through. When the first imported iron bark shingles were brought from Sydney in August 1823 the settlers were at last able to ensure dry homes for themselves.

It is not until the Williams arrival in August 1823 that it is possible to turn from the practical and economic difficulties of building the Mission House. We can glimpse, through extracts copied late last century from Marianne Williams' original diaries, a picture of domestic life within and around its walls. Marianne Williams stayed with the Butlers for five weeks. Rounding Kororipo Point into the basin, the Mission House had looked to Marianne Williams like stone or stucco. "But" she wrote "it was built of wood painted white, and lined with plank within and finished in a superior manner to the wooden houses in Hampstead." She made particular note of her first midday dinner at the Butlers of soup, fish, ham, vegetables and pudding. Thirteen adults and ten children sat down to a meal a day or so later at the Kemp home, feasting on chicken, ham, pigeons and roast pork, followed by baked custard and a tart of preserved quince.

On the first night in the Butler home she saw her children 'comfortably asleep in the whare karakia, our ship-mattresses and bedding spread upon the carpet . . .' The whare karakia was the sitting room, so named as it was used for prayers at this time. It is now called the parlour. A door led from this room to one of the small eight foot by eight foot rooms on the ends of the verandah. While the children slept, Mrs Williams and Mrs Butler 'were glad to draw near the comfortable wood-fire, made upon the hearth, like the kitchens in Norfolk farm-houses or in cottages in Oxfordshire', while the men of the mission held a meeting across the hall in the dining room.

Next day Mrs Williams sorted out a chest and trunks of linen and visited the Kemps. In the days following, Mrs Butler showed her how she managed her pigs, poultry, rabbits, pigeons, goats and turkeys. Mrs Butler's cow was not in milk yet, but she was able to make Irish butter from goats' milk. For Sunday midday dinner, the whare karakia was transformed after service into a dining room for the occasion. In the afternoon a service was held for the natives in the kitchen outhouse. Mrs Williams was full of praise for the native servants whom she said were 'superior in manner and activity to my English born and Port Jackson reared little maid'. (This 'little maid' was to cause considerable trouble later on.) Mrs Butler insisted on having all the Williams' soiled linen washed by two hired native girls who were paid each with a hoe for every four washes. All the servant girls in the house were paid three monthly, as was the boy who minded the goats, one quarter with axes and the following with hoes.

It was a tranquil first week. The folding of the wash and the ironing were all that Mrs Butler would allow the pregnant Marianne Williams to do. But as 'Mrs Butler's eyes were so bad, and her constantly bustling life left no time for the needle', Mrs Williams gladly stitched for her, taking her work basket and the children to the Kemp home. At the Kemps the children had their lessons. When freed from these, they found play with the waggon and wheelbarrows a great source of delight.

At others times the children played in the partly enclosed verandah of the Butler home. They acquired head lice, wrote Mrs Williams, from time to time from visiting native children but she dealt with these with equanimity. 'I am always informed of it by their sudden and vehement scratching of their heads; and by the constant application of a small tooth-comb this evil is immediately stopped.'

After a time, Mrs Williams was longing to join her husband who was building their raupo house at Paihia. The Butlers were pressing her not to go, or if she did, to return to Kerikeri for her confinement. The comfort and kindness, she wrote, with which she was continually meeting seemed to her quite too much.

Her pert maid Betsy was another matter. The native servant Jane (who was a cousin of Hongi Hika) became ill, and it was found that Betsy had given her peppermint essence from a bottle stolen from their supplies, which she hid in the glass bookcase in the whare karakia. They found later that Betsy had also stolen from drawers in this room some English print, a

silver knife and some silver money, all keepsakes of Butler's children. Betsy was punished for her hurt to Jane by being locked up for the day, despite her tearful pleading upon her knees. Then it was discovered she had 'the itch'. Her saucy reply to this revelation was that she had caught it while with the Williams. There was nothing to do then but confine her until she could be sent back to New South Wales in the care of the Wesleyan Leighs who would be going back on the *Brampton*. Marianne Williams left Kerikeri to join her husband at Paihia in the middle of September and in November 1823 the Butlers left Kerikeri for good.

Unfortunately we do not have any detailed diary entries to tell us how the rooms of the Mission House looked from 1822 until 1832 when the Kemps moved in. We know that the wood lining was bright with whitewash and that shutters closed the lower windows in times of trouble. The windows may have been curtained. The Rev. John Butler may have brought back silk or damask from New South Wales in early 1822. But, with shutters to close at night, simple muslin hung across the windows would have given privacy in the daytime. Blind holland is recorded as being in the stores in 1828 and may have been available earlier. It is also possible that some of the materials sent out for use as clothing may have been used for curtaining, such as indian print, brown, blue, striped or checked cottons, though with these earmarked for shirts for the New Zealanders this is perhaps unlikely.

Furnishing would have varied with the personal possessions of the

The Mission House

Kerikeri, Bay of Islands in 1858. The old Baker house has been rented from the Church Missionary Society by James Kemp, but by the time the Rev. John Kinder painted this picture it was almost in ruins. The Stone Store has lost its belfry and the original 1819 buildings are gone, finally demolished some time between 1856 and 1858.
ALEXANDER TURNBULL LIBRARY

occupants. Furniture which was the property of the Church Missionary Society and remained in the house when the Butler family left consisted of two tables, a washstand, a sideboard, three sofas, twelve chairs, two of which were elbow chairs, and a bedstead. Four years after George Clarke and his wife and child moved into the 'ready furnished' house in 1824, the sitting room was said to have had in it a small carpet, eight chairs, a table and a sofa, with maps hung about the walls. Maps seem to have been a favourite way of relieving the starkness of the whitewashed walls.

Four-poster beds, popular in England at the time, were not uncommon in New Zealand, even in the earliest days. The curtained surrounds, great draught stoppers in homes which often were not wind or even watertight, would have afforded privacy in rooms which were sometimes shared with children. Both the Halls and the Kings at Rangihoua had four-posters when the mission started in 1814. Chintz piece goods, probably from India, blue or tea coloured backgrounds with a small running pattern, and lined with material of the background colour, dressed missionary beds in the early 1830s. The early panelled bed which is now in the front upstairs single bedroom of the Kemp House, is a four-poster type bed with truncated posts. Linen sheets, and blankets would probably have been topped with a white counterpane. Flax mats covered the tops of tables, chests and boxes in this room in 1841. Flax matting, which was practical and readily replaceable, may have also been used to protect carpet squares and in areas of heavy use.

Five dozen white chamber pots ordered in 1832 would have put this convenience under every mission bed or in a side commode. A pewter bed pan also served in cases of illness. Blue and white china and heavy cream coloured Bristol ware was set upon huckaback tablecloths for everyday family dinners. Huckaback tea towels dried the china after the washing up. A shower bath installed in the late 1820s, possibly in the kitchen outhouse, seemed to be looked upon as an aid to better health, rather than for routine cleanliness. Copper boilers, in general use for the family wash, became the receptacle on at least one occasion for the brewing of beer from homegrown hops. The New Zealanders had long made a juice from the tutuwai berries, but the missionaries went a step further, turning this juice into tupakihi wine which they used at celebrations such as a mission wedding. Coffee and quantities of tea were drunk as well as porter. This last could also be used as a leaven in place of yeast — a teaspoon of sugar, six teaspoons of flour and a little porter in a bottle, with sugar and water added from time to time to keep the 'bug' going. Spirits seem to have been used only for medicinal purposes. The early medicine chests had the basics of calico, styptic, castor oil, rhubarb, bassilican, zinc ointment and essence of peppermint. A cupping machine was considered essential. Wounds were occasionally dressed with potato scrapings. Bleeding was frequently resorted to in dire illness. The mission children were all vaccinated for smallpox in 1828. A treat for the children in 1824 was a box of sugar candy sent from England. Ginger tea and biscuits satisfied their parents, and dried apples from the American ships, when available, added relish to the constant diet of pork.

The women had sprigged muslin for their dresses in summer and in 1822 Mrs Kemp and Mrs Butler wore brown or purple twill. Bombazine, twilled with silk or cotton, usually black, would have been Sunday best. Gene (jean), white with purple or pink stripes, was popular along with glazed cottons. The little girls were no doubt dressed in similar materials while the little boys wore short jackets buttoned to their trousers with metal buttons. On one exceedingly hot January day in 1825, Mrs Williams, who was staying with her children at Kerikeri, stripped her son Henry down 'to one single garment which he managed to get off, and to his great delight ran about naked'.

White cotton caps were worn daily by the women and Mrs Williams wrote that the Kerikeri River water was excellent for whitening them. Hats or bonnets for summer were leghorn or panama for both men and women. In winter the mission men wore black beaver hats to top off their dark suits of fustian and carried with them the useful umbrella. Nankeen, a yellow cotton cloth, was commonly used for waistcoats. The boat cloak, an essential item in the early days, was replaced later by a top coat. Lamb's wool stockings warmed their legs in winter when sleeping out of doors or in tents on their frequent journeys away from home. Shoes were a problem in the earliest days. James Shepherd made many of these for the settlement as well as trousers for the New Zealanders who were then clamouring for European clothing. Quantities of shoes in all sizes were later imported, to fit the feet of the growing crowd of mission children.

At the end of the eventful year of 1823, which saw the arrival of the Rev. Henry Williams and his family, the dismissal of the Rev. Thomas Kendall and the removal of the Butler family to New South Wales, the Mission House stood empty awaiting the arrival from Sydney of the missionary schoolmaster George Clarke. James Shepherd, whose family quarters were in the Butlers' old rooms at the end of the storehouse, slept in the Mission House at night to protect it. There had been threats after Butler left that it would be set on fire. Investigating unusual sounds one night, Shepherd discovered the chief Hihi perched on one of the beams of the barn. Throwing a quantity of harness down to entangle Shepherd he leapt from the beam. The agile Shepherd escaped through a window, the chief in pursuit. After Shepherd had fled, Hihi resumed his plunder, taking several articles of husbandry, the yard dog, and leaving a shattered window. Following this scuffle, Shepherd moved his family into the Mission House.

The threat also hung over the mission of Hongi bringing his friend Kendall up to Kerikeri to put him in the house. Shepherd endured many taunts from the chiefs. Asked scornfully by the chief Pakira when he intended to move to the raupo house built for him by 'Towee' at Parengaroa, Shepherd defensively replied in Hongi's presence that he would remain where he was as Mr Butler's house was becoming his. Shepherd was confident that he and his family would live in the Mission House, even if they shared it with George Clarke when he came. He was a good deal surprised to find that Clarke, who stayed with the Kemps on his arrival in March 1824, wanted it to himself. Shepherd thought there was an abundance of room for both families, especially if it were partitioned. Told by the committee of missionaries that if he should be unwilling to leave the house they would write to Mr Marsden, Shepherd reluctantly moved back to his old quarters, partly mollified by the promise of having the outside kitchen joined to the store building with a study off the resulting passage. George Clarke, his wife and baby son, moved into the Mission House in May 1824, just after the worst flood of many which raged down the Kerikeri River had swept away the fence around the cowyard by the river and part of the fence which enclosed the house.

In August 1824, the farmer Richard Davis, his wife and what George Clarke termed their 'interesting family' of five children crowded into the Mission House with the Clarkes. Although very welcome there, the Davis family must have put considerably more pressure on the space than Shepherd would have done. Davis' presence in the house also brought further threats to burn down the building. As in Butler's time, this arose from the New Zealanders' knowledge of letters written by Davis to Marsden. Spoken criticism by the missionaries of a chief's behaviour could be treated with scorn, but the writing down of his name in a letter or book was an act which stole from that chief his mana and, consequently, the mana of his tribe. To defend his mana, the chief had to extract utu.

Davis had insisted that he must enter the chief Moka's name in his records as having stolen a sheep. Furthermore it had come to Moka's ears that Davis had written about him to England. Threats were made that Davis would be stripped, or worse, and that the Mission House would be pulled down. A direct result of Davis' letter was an incident in October 1824, when the chief Tinana rushed into the schoolroom (the outhouse kitchen was used for Clarke's native school) and attempted to go into the house on the pretext of wanting a girl slave who had allegedly compared her rangatira husband to a dog. The house door, hurriedly shut, was struck with a large piece of wood from the adjacent woodheap, and in short order the backyard was filled with New Zealanders. All seems to have ended without more trouble but in November Clarke was threatened with a hatchet. Seeing he was not alarmed, the man took out his anger on a couple of passing ducks, chopping the head off one.

Fighting schoolboys almost caused an angry mob to plunder the house. Clarke separated them, leading one boy through the gate by the river. The irate boy promptly sat down in the water and refused to budge. The cry went up that Clarke was drowning the boy and in a moment he was surrounded. Again the situation was calmed, but Clarke remarked, 'I can see how ready they are to make an attack on us'.

Davis' letter was one reason for the Maori anger; he had, in addition, chosen the land of their enemy Te Morenga for a farm. He was no better, in their view, than Shepherd. The Davis' presence in the house put the property at risk, but according to James Kemp the vendetta against Davis was not the only factor in his leaving Kerikeri for Paihia only months after his arrival there. Clarke had said that he did not want Davis to stay on in his house, and if he was to remain at Kerikeri he would have to live elsewhere as he needed room for a school. Davis had been very much hurt by this, although the house must have been very crowded. With Davis gone, the Clarkes remained reasonably peacefully in the house for the next six years, having it to themselves except for occasional visits from the Paihia and Rangihoua brethren with their wives and families, and also the Wesleyans. Mrs Clarke, whose health was fragile, was a courageous woman much loved by all.

The Mission House garden, so carefully laid out by the Rev. John Butler, was a joy to Clarke who wrote to his father in November 1827 describing it.

> *I should like dr Father very much if you could now take a walk in my Garden which Abounds with* Grapes, Lemons, Apples, peaches, Raspberries, currans, Strawberries *and I know not what which will be all ripe in the course of 3 months. In another year or two I shall have plenty of* Oranges *and* pears. *I have also a Walnut tree growing and a Number of Plumb trees: We are enjoying one of the most Salubrious climates in the* World.

The Clarkes acquired a boarder in January 1828 in the person of the Rev. William Yate, who slept in one of the small verandah rooms. It was probably the one off the sitting room, being more private than that off the dining room, and the sitting room could also have been used for writing and study. The unsatisfactory shingles on the Mission House roof were letting rain in, and Yate had to have tubs and pails scattered about his little room during a downpour.

The mission families at all the settlements were increasing in size and the children needed more schooling than their parents had time or talent to give. The Rev. A.N. Brown was expected in New Zealand and he was to start his Boys' School at Kerikeri. The Rev. William Yate had already begun a school for the Kerikeri boys and enthusiastic plans were made to have a 'seminary' built on the large flat area across the Kerikeri River which would be bridged. In the meantime a temporary house would be built for the Rev. Brown, and the new chapel which was being built in 1828 could serve as his schoolroom. Yate, while on a visit to New South Wales, went ahead and ordered the bricks for the seminary.

However, there was a change of plans in March 1830. Clarke and Yate were to go to the proposed Waimate Station, while Brown would move into the Mission House and conduct his Boys' School there. In August 1830, Alfred Nisbet, a Scottish carpenter who had come to New Zealand in 1823 with the first New Zealand Company, was employed to renovate the Mission House for Brown's use, working on it for the next few months. Clarke had already shifted into his temporary home at Waimate, when in March 1831 the decision was made for Brown to remain at Paihia, with a new arrival Thomas Chapman directed to move immediately into the Mission House. Clarke wrote bitterly that he had only agreed to an early removal to Waimate because he was confident that Brown would be at Kerikeri. The persuasiveness of the Williams brothers' letters to the Society in London had at last convinced that body that Paihia was the most suitable place for Schoolmaster Brown. Perhaps what tipped the balance were William Williams' strong words on the value he and his brother Henry placed on Latin and Greek (which Brown refused to teach, forcing the Williams to keep their children at Paihia and teach them themselves).

When Chapman shifted into the Mission House in March 1831 the leaky roof had probably been repaired by Nisbet with iron-bark shingles shipped from Australia. Nisbet continued to work intermittently on the house until early 1832. In the middle of 1832 the Kemps and the Chapmans exchanged houses. It has always been said that the skilling (the whole of the lean-to part of the house) had been put up in 1834 when James Kemp reported putting up a frame for a skilling/kitchen. But other documentary evidence suggested that the skilling had been built in two parts, and following the floods of 1981 this was found to be so. The first part built appears to have been the kitchen and 'pantry' which gave on to a small porch outside the back door of the original house. It is possible that this first part was in fact built some time between the end of 1831 and the end of 1832. The skilling as it is today with kitchen, pantry, passages, storeroom and two other rooms was probably not finished completely until 1836. A door which had been boarded over between the dining room and kitchen was also discovered in 1981, and this has now been restored.

Visitors to the house today will find the dining room painted a dull yellow. A coat of this colour paint over the original whitewash was also suspected and found in 1981. 'Patent yellow', 'Stone oker' and 'Prussian blue' were imported in 1833, colourful additions to the standard black, white and red previously received.

The kitchen/outhouse may have been used in 1830 to house the first printing press brought to New Zealand by William Yate. Decaying even then, it was probably demolished in 1832 to make way for the carpenter's shop and forge put up for the building of the Stone Store. The shop and forge were still standing in the middle of this century, but the site is now occupied by the Curator's home. The skilling of Kemp House also covers part of the site of the original kitchen outhouse.

Felton Mathew, the Acting Government Surveyor, visited the Mission House in February 1840 and wrote that the building was 'so screened by trees as not to be perceptible from the River . . . It is a somewhat comfortless wooden house, but from being so thickly surrounded by trees and flowering shrubs, has a picturesque and comfortable appearance.' Adding to the trees which had been planted by Butler in 1820 and 1821 were the now well-grown fruit trees in an orchard planted by James Kemp in 1834 where the stockyard by the river had been. This orchard was said to be 'very pretty' by Lady Franklin, wife of the Governor of Tasmania, in 1841, but of the house she wrote that it was a 'dingy mission dwelling embowered also in its wattles and briar roses with a verandah of a most

The Mission House

uninviting appearance.' Lady Franklin and Felton Mathew may have been better pleased with its appearance at the end of 1843. In that year it had been thoroughly repaired at very heavy expense. The 'uninviting' verandah with its two small rooms was demolished and a narrower verandah wrapped around three sides of the house was added, giving it the balanced and charming appearance it has today.

The Kemp family had been living in the Mission House from 1832, but after receiving approval in 1859, Kemp exchanged Kororipo Point with the Church Missionary Society for the house and three acres around it. From 1860, when he took title, the old Mission House could truly be called 'Kemp House' as it is known today. Many minor changes were made to the house to accommodate succeeding generations of the Kemp family. These changes included the addition of a wash-house in 1926. In 1976 the old Kemp home was given into the care of the Historic Places Trust by Ernest Kemp, a great-grandson of the pioneer missionaries James and Charlotte Kemp.

Kemp House in the later years of last century. James Kemp Jnr is standing on the verandah.
HOCKEN LIBRARY

The Kemp House and the Stone Store, Kerikeri, in December 1844. The new verandah to the Mission House (Kemp House) was built in 1843. Behind the house is Kemp's blacksmith shop, built in 1832. Left middle is the former house of William Parrott. The bell tower on the Stone Store was finished in 1834. John Edmonds built the 'temporary' stone pier in 1838. In the foreground are two of the original Kerikeri buildings: the storehouse (right), built in 1819, and James Kemp's first house, 1820. The picture is from the W.C. Cotton Journal.
DIXSON LIBRARY, SYDNEY

The second chapel at Kerikeri built 1828–29 and replaced by St James' Church in 1878. The original of this picture was painted in ink and watercolour by T.B. Hutton in 1844 and is found in W.C. Cotton's Journal.
DIXSON LIBRARY, SYDNEY

Section 2

Chapel, Schoolhouse and Church

'Our church will be sixty feet long, by thirty-four feet wide,' declared the Rev. John Butler in the first flush of missionary fervour, 'this, perhaps will be sufficient for a few years . . .' He and William Hall of Rangihoua had marked out a site on a small eminence above the Kerikeri Basin that morning, 6 October 1819. Nearby was to be a school, a large sixty by eighteen foot building.

This eminence has now been cut through by the road up the hill. The original site chosen was probably more to the centre of this gentle hill, closer to where the Rev. John Butler would be building his house, rather than on the edge of the steep slope to the Waitotorongo Creek where the present church stands. In spite of Butler's confidence in 1819, no church, chapel or school was built for four years, and then not on the hill.

In the first months of settlement, services with native 'congregations' were held out of doors. The services and prayer meetings for settlers were in their unfinished rooms. Not all the settlers attended these. That the carpenters were walking out 'to take their pleasure' and purchasing pigs on a Sunday was noted critically by James Shepherd. By September 1820 the raupo-thatched and unlined blacksmith's shop which had been the Kemps' and Francis Hall's first home became a 'temporary church'. This building, the first built at Kerikeri, had a reading desk made for it by the end of the year; and when the first wheat was got in, hymns were sung in the sweet-smelling chapel, the now-shingled loft of which doubled as a barn. In this oven-hot loft Francis Hall had sweated through summer and been doused by rain in the winter.

The Rev. John Butler saw his grand plans for a church set aside in the face of the realities of his situation — his lack of control of the carpenters, the difficulties of getting sufficient timber without trading in guns, and perhaps above all his overwhelming need to build a house for himself first. After nine months at Kerikeri he informed the Society that he thought it would be a long time before either a church or school would be built. In October 1821, when there was a prospect of his house being built, he turned his thoughts to a church briefly, writing that he would not rest until a church was built.

The old blacksmith's shop remained the church for the settlement until Butler's home was almost finished in early 1822. Francis Hall wrote despairingly in April of that year, when he was being accused by Butler of thwarting Butler's efforts to build a school, 'He is unstable as water in all his ways except one — and that is, <u>his own interest</u>, and in this particular he is as steady and as faithful as the Needle to the North.' Butler, he added, was now 'red-hot' about a school but it wouldn't last. In fact Butler had built a large barn by the end of 1822. In early 1823 the settlers seemed as far away from having a chapel built as ever. Butler was holding morning and evening prayer for the natives in his outhouse kitchen and European services within his home. He seems to have been conducting his native services independently of other missionaries, for in January 1823 Shepherd asked him, 'would it not be much to our comfort and union to meet altogether?' adding that he thought the enclosed verandah of Butler's house should suit well. Butler disapproved, telling Shepherd that when his old barn was free of Shepherd's wheat it would suit very well. This old barn was a thirty by ten foot structure which had walls and roof of raupo. On a Sabbath afternoon in February 1823 the first native school class was held in this flimsy building. Shepherd complained that although Butler was nominally Superintendent, it fell upon him to instruct the thirty New Zealanders attending, as Butler and Kemp were not skilled in the language. Shepherd's criticism of the place in which the school was held was countered by Butler who told him that if he had not gone into the rooms at the end of the old store when Butler had moved out of them into the house, they would have served the purpose very well.

With no encouragement from the native school superintendent to build a school, Kemp and Shepherd set off to the Kawakawa to get spars, determined to build one themselves. The timber was got up to Kerikeri in March. School attendance had lapsed by the time Shepherd joined the Wesleyans to go to Whangaroa in May, and without Shepherd the school could not be revived. Although timber was earmarked for a school, none had been used when the Rev. Samuel Marsden arrived at Kerikeri in August 1823. One of the reasons for Marsden's insistence on cutting down the size of Sam Butler's house to be built at the proposed new station at Toharanui was to conserve some of the timber in hand for its intended purpose — the building of a school cum chapel. Forced to stay on in New Zealand after the wreck of the *Brampton*, Marsden wrote in his journal:

> *I am determined that the missionaries shall begin to erect a school at Kiddee-kiddee the next week. Should I be obliged to remain two months I hope to see it completed and the children admitted into it.*

Kemp and Shepherd, he said, had readily complied with his request.

A flagstaff made of a spar was set up on 2 October 1823 to mark the spot, and part of the frame went up the following day. Kemp was appointed by Marsden to have the building of the 'Public School' entirely under his direction. The missionary George Clarke would be coming soon as school teacher to replace Francis Hall who would be leaving New Zealand. The Rev. John Butler was extremely angry at what he saw as disregard of his son's needs. Forced to comply with Marsden's wishes, he had two of his native sawyers and a European worker fence along the front of the chapel site, closing the gap between the fence round Butler's garden and house and the fence which surrounded the group of buildings on the Waitotorongo Creek.

The frame of the twenty-five by sixteen foot school/chapel was up by November 1823 and a mud wall for a skillion to it had been started at the back. It was, wrote Kemp

> *in the senter (sic) of the settlement and in a public situation. It being the first building that has been erected in this settlement for the establishing of religious worship amongst the natives.*

The building was still not ready for use when Samuel Marsden with Butler, now suspended from office, and his family went back to New South Wales. School for the male New Zealanders was held in the outhouse kitchen of the Mission House (Butler's) until March 1824, by which time William Puckey Snr had laid the floor of the school/chapel.

Three lamps were fetched from the stores to light the rooms and on 11 April 1824 the first native service was held in their new school/chapel. The large bell intended for a chapel at Rangihoua for the Rev. Thomas Kendall had been returned to Kerikeri following Kendall's dismissal and was probably set up in a wooden frame nearby. This was the settlement 'clock' marking the hours when struck for work and prayer. (A clock had been in the stores since at least 1822, but there was still nowhere to place it.)

The schoolmaster George Clarke, his wife and son came to Kerikeri in time to take part in the blessing of the building on 19 April when all the brethren from Rangihoua and Paihia were present. James Kemp preached at the native services, but it was 'painful to be a witness to it' recorded Clarke,

> *Some would be cutting the boards others would be making faces and mimicing Mr Kemp some would hiss him, others laugh and another would contradict what was said others would burst into laughter some would lie down on the seats to sleep.*

William Puckey Jnr later recalled an old cock being thrown in at the window by grimacing, spitting New Zealanders. Only a few days after the opening of the chapel, boards were torn off the back.

The novelty of the building and the interest in a school for their children soon wore off, although the first Girls' School started by the devout Mrs Clarke had some success. The New Zealanders continued to mock the missionary efforts to convert them, spurred sometimes by Hongi's avowed distaste for European karakia. Many New Zealanders thought that to be called 'lambs' of God was low and degrading. Often there were great crowds of New Zealanders about the chapel stopping the settlers from using it at all. Not fenced to the rear, it stood in an open field with goats and sheep grazing around it.

In September 1824 the first Christian burial of a New Zealander at Kerikeri took place when 'Wattoo' — 'a brand plucked from the burning' — who had lived with George Clarke for three months in New South Wales, died and was laid to rest in a deal coffin in a grave behind the chapel, 'to await the sound of the Archangel's trumpet, when all that are in their graves shall hear and come forth, to give their account.' The New Zealanders came the following day to perform their own rituals at their countryman's resting place.

Attendance at the schools waxed and waned over the following years, depending on a sufficiency of food to feed the scholars, or on the whim of the parents who took them away on any pretext. It was not uncommon for chiefs to ask to be 'payed' when their children were attending. One of the ideas for keeping the school children amused and exercised was to import from England in 1821 about 100 battledores with shuttlecocks, some of which were given out about a year later and again in 1826. 'Bird calls' and Jews harps were also part of the school equipment, along with utilitarian tin cans, pewter plates, earthern mugs and saucers, slates, thread and needles, knitting needles and wool, sets of cards for teaching letters, and 'Books as are used in the National School'. Striped, checked woven or printed cloth came for the children's clothing.

Clarke the schoolmaster could joyfully report in mid 1826 that

> *instead of seeing 4 or 5 poor distressed creatures dressed in dirty Native Mats sitting upon the seats of the Chapel with their feet drawn under them we have the pleasure of seeing and addressing 40, and sometimes more, attentive and clean Natives all in European clothes.*

It would be a mistake to think that the New Zealanders had European dress forced upon them. There is no doubt in those early days it was much desired, although often worn in an imaginative fashion.

When the Rev. William Yate came to Kerikeri to take charge of the settlement at the beginning of 1828, the schools were flourishing. The schoolhouse/chapel itself was looking more settled with trees about it which James Kemp had planted the previous year. It was within the chapel yard that Yate began to build his house, to which he hoped he would one day bring his beloved sister, and planted his garden.

Yate began the practice of keeping the chapel door open during Sunday and inviting New Zealanders passing through the settlement to enter. Fifty or sixty men, women, boys and girls were now attending the schools and a congregation of a hundred on Sundays was not uncommon. A larger building was needed. It was decided that the old chapel should be taken down and a new one rebuilt in the same place by the Basin. But when the building was demolished, it was found that the ground plates were so decayed that they could not be re-used. It was agreed to build an entirely new chapel on the hill behind the houses. In

T.B. Hutton executed this ink and watercolour picture 'At chapel' in 1844. William Bambridge, attending chapel around this time, commented 'D[ea]r Willy was remarkably troublesome; perhaps he disapproved of having hose on. I was obliged to take him outside and correct his foolishness'. The picture comes from the W.C. Cotton Journal.
DIXSON LIBRARY, SYDNEY

November of 1828 the Clarke's baby daughter died of whooping cough. Laid in a tiny coffin with a rose from the Mission House garden in her hand, she was buried in what was to be the cemetery of the yet unbuilt chapel.

The large barn which Butler had built in 1822 was cleared out for a temporary schoolroom, although it also was in such a bad state that it could not be used when it rained. The new building, spoken of as a schoolroom and 'temporary' chapel, was designed by George Clarke. Begun in November 1828 it took nearly eight months to build and the first native prayers were held in it in June 1829. The main body of the building was thirty-eight feet by eighteen feet, with a skilling twelve feet by eleven feet attached 'for the convenience of a fire'. It was constructed of lath and plaster (buying timber from the New Zealanders was too expensive at this time) and at the grand opening on 8 December 1829 it had been plastered and whitewashed inside and out. James Hamlin had made seats for it, and the church clock was at long last taken out of the stores and placed in the front gable.

The great day came when the huihinga — in missionary terms the public examination of the work and learning of the Maori school children from all the mission settlements, followed by a feast — was to be celebrated. The contingent from Paihia and Rangihoua, coming up the Kerikeri Inlet in flag-bedecked canoes and boats, went ashore to change from workaday clothes to Sunday best before the grand arrival in the Kerikeri Basin. Mrs Marianne Williams recorded the excitement of the Maori and Pakeha children:

> *When we opened upon the settlement, we were all, seven in number abreast, all paddling in unison . . . . The boys dressed in white shirts and trowsers and scotch caps; the Kiddee Kiddee lads in the same assembled in the landing-place. All voices were hushed . . . The song or chant of the native paddlers was first low, and swelled and increased in vehemence to the utmost as we advanced . . . and then the loud English hurra of the boys on the landing-place was instantly answered by a sudden burst of every voice in the boats standing up and waving their caps. The children were in ecstasies and we were well nigh deafened.*

Examinations of handiwork — sewing and carpentry — and the service over, 200 Maori school children sat down to the feast. Stirabout, 300lbs of flour and 100lbs of sugar boiled with water was consumed. Nine axes and 44 leghorn hats were distributed as prizes. Tea was taken in Mr Yate's garden by the adults and the boys 'like so many wild colts had a scamper up and down the frame of Mr Yate's new house'.

By the middle of the following year a 'road' had been made up to the chapel and towards the end of the year Baker was building his permanent lath and plaster house nearby from the frame of Yate's dismantled house down by the Basin. Yate, who would go to Waimate, was occupied with the first printing press. First off the press was a hymn which was sung in the chapel in September 1830.

A raupo house for Charles Baker, the nurseryman, had already been built on the hill when it was decided to erect the church nearby. As a consequence, the chapel was probably not on the site which Butler had selected in 1819. There was no porch on the chapel building in 1829, but this may have been added in March 1831 when the front, which had fallen down, was repaired. At this time also the clock may have been removed for safety. It would later be placed in the belfry of the Stone Store.

Ten years later, in 1841, Lady Franklin described the schoolroom-chapel:

> *The church is a cleanly-looking modest building of lath & plaster, its white walls being relieved by the green frames of its windows & the green verandah in front of the entrance door — a window on each side of this entrance & three on each side of the building give light to the interior which is also very neatly plastered. It has a pulpit opposite the entrance door & behind this a small room for robing . . . .*

Lady Franklin may have been charmed by the building's simplicity, but not so Capt. Fitzroy who in 1835 did not like being told that what he had thought was a 'respectable' church, was the Stone Store and that the 'small low edifice' on the hill was a place of worship. The Church Missionary Society in London was mortified by Fitzroy's comments in his book published in 1840, and wrote to the missionaries chiding them for having a chapel in 'disadvantageous contrast' with other buildings. Buildings set apart for public worship should, consistent of course with economy, 'bear a character soberly in accordance with the object to which they are appropriate'.

But by the time this stricture was received, Kerikeri was no longer the heart of the Bay of Islands mission stations. There was no money to waste on a new church. Fitzroy had been correct when he said it looked more like a small schoolhouse than a church, for that had been the primary intention; and as a chapel for worship it was quite in accord with the concepts of the low church evangelists.

William Bambridge, on holiday from Bishop Selwyn's St John's College at Waimate in 1844, attended Sunday service in the chapel. He found, he said, the service very little different from prayers in the chapel on workdays. There was no sermon and no chanting. School was held in the chapel every morning, when Bambridge made sketches of several of the Maori students.

By the end of 1848, Mary Taua, the faithful Christian infant teacher and friend of the Kemps since the early years of the mission, had been laid to rest in the graveyard. Here also lay two Kemp infants and the Clarkes' little girl, their graves embowered in fragrant honeysuckle. Thirty years later, in 1878, the great Ngati Rehia chief Pakira (half-brother of the immense Tareha) was buried here, his headstone recording his age as ninety. These old chiefs, who had once been so opposed to the missionaries' God, had embraced Christianity, but not all who did so found their final resting place in a church burial ground. Hone Heke had taken the remains of the converted Tareha to a Maori burial place. By then instead of a body resting at Kororipo Point on its last journey inland, it was sometimes placed in the chapel.

In the late 1860s rampant bracken surrounding the chapel was a fire hazard, and the building had lost its porch. The fragile lath and plaster structure had served for over fifty years as schoolhouse and chapel. In 1878 it was replaced by a 'remarkably neat little church' which was dedicated on 5 December 1878. The ceremony was followed by a feast of meat, fish, oyster patties, huge plum puddings and cakes, all spread on tables placed in the shade of two 'gigantic' old pear trees.

Chapel had become Church — one which would have satisfied both Fitzroy and the Church Missionary Society. Now, with its harmonious 1963 additions the church is well over a hundred years old, settled tranquilly on the hill where New Zealand's first resident clergyman, the Rev. John Butler, had hoped it would be.

Kerikeri, probably in the 1880s. The present St James' Church sits on its hilltop site where the Rev. John Butler had hoped a church would stand.
HOCKEN LIBRARY, DUNEDIN

Section 3

The Stone Store and Mill

The proposal to build the Stone Store was mooted at a time when the missionaries were uneasy brothers. There were conflicting options on whether the Rev. A.N. Brown should be stationed at Kerikeri or Paihia; whether Rangihoua should be shifted to Te Puna or abandoned; whether the mission farm at Waimate should be started or the southward missions undertaken. These major differences of opinion aroused such angry and bitter feelings in the brethren's breasts over the years 1830-34 that it is a wonder the Stone Store was built at all. Henry Williams of Paihia turned out to be right when he wrote in 1835 that the still unfinished store had been a waste of money and missionary strength. The Rev. William Yate, having the sympathetic ear of Samuel Marsden and the Corresponding Committee of the Society on his visits to New South Wales, had carried the day.

Marsden had long wanted a water mill at Kerikeri. On every visit he made to the Bay of Islands, from 1814 on, he advocated the erection of a mill which would grind the corn and wheat which the New Zealanders grew. With only small inefficient hand mills they became discouraged. And they had found that there was much less labour and greater profit in growing potatoes for trade with the ships. But a mill would also benefit a mission farm when eventually established. The 1824 plans for a farm at inland Taiamai under the charge of the farmer Richard Davis had come to nothing. A plan to put a mill at Waipapa a few miles down the Kerikeri Inlet, near where Marsden had proposed first James Shepherd (1823), and then William Williams (1826), might be stationed, had also failed. Confident that a mill would be built at either Kerikeri or Waipapa, the Society had sent had sent out with Farmer Davis in 1824 a pair of the best French Burr millstones.

In the years after that enthusiastic agriculturist, the Rev. John Butler, had left the mission late in 1823, the stores had been brought from New South Wales either by the shipping or the mission ship *Herald*. The *Herald* also bartered for food around the coasts. All supplies were off-loaded at the Paihia Station. Sometimes the *Herald* would take what was needed at Kerikeri to within four or five miles of the settlement, from where the supplies would be ferried up river by canoe or in the mission's small boat. Usually it took a week to get supplies, sailing and rowing the small boat, from Paihia to Kerikeri.

The old wooden building which housed the mission stores, as well various families from 1819, was much decayed eleven years later and there was the ever present danger from fire with raupo kitchens and huts attached to the timber structure. There had already been alarms when chimneys had set fire to the thatch of the kitchens.

While the Rev. William Yate of Kerikeri was in New South Wales in the first half of 1830 the committee of missionaries passed a resolution to build a forty feet by twenty feet store house at Paihia. This project was abandoned after Marsden, on a visit in March 1830, directed that a mission farm under Davis, Clarke and Hamlin be established at Waimate. Kerikeri was the key, as Kemp wrote, to the successful operation of the farm. Wheat grown at the model farm would be brought down by dray and ground in the mill to be built there.

Marsden, after his return to New South Wales at the end of May 1830, had the Corresponding Committee get estimates for a mill within a few weeks. Approval had come from the society by July (Marsden had long before written of his proposals) with the anxious qualification that it could be done only if it was without serious expense. It seems probable, too, that consideration had been given at the time of Marsden's visit to the suitability of the old store to house grain. James Hamlin and his family would be quitting their rooms there when the time came to remove to Waimate, but other workmen might have to be housed in it if a new store was to be built. The Kerikeri missionaries sat tight. Until Waimate was habitable there was no need to press the necessity.

With the removal of Clarke, Yate and Hamlin to Waimate in early 1831, immediate attention was given to building a new store and mill. A case containing the collar, bridle and harness for the mill works had already arrived when James Kemp made his plea for a new store at the April 1831 quarterly meeting of missionaries. He drew attention to the insecure state of the old store. The uprights, weatherboards and other parts were completely decayed and 'the whole of the Society's property being therefore exposed to the natives should they be inclined to pilfer.'

Kemp made a good case, and despite rumbles from Paihia it was resolved that the old store was to be repaired until a more suitable one could be erected. One thousand feet of timber was to be bought from Styles and Harris timberyard at Hokianga.

Perhaps Henry Williams hoped it would stop there — with repairs to the existing store — but it seems fairly certain that the Kerikeri people, supported by Yate, already had a Stone Store in mind, as did Marsden. The solidity and permanence of stone walls represented the best of English building practice. They could be made proof against rats and would greatly diminish the fire hazard. Thomas Chapman at Kerikeri, thought that a steel windmill would be better for Kerikeri, with a water mill built later at Waimate, but by September 1831 the stonemason, William Parrott, had already been contracted in New South Wales to do the stonework. Henry Williams was away in the mission cutter *Karere* in October 1831 when the committee of missionaries resolved to use this vessel on its return to bring local stone from down the Kerikeri Inlet up to the store site. Henry Williams on his return was so angered by this decision that the rift which had existed between the Paihia and Kerikeri brethren was widened to the extent that Henry Williams was to refuse to allow the Kerikeri and Waimate people to land stores, including stones for the Stone Store from New South Wales, at Paihia. Marsden, he wrote, by some magical power had so influenced the minds of the members at Kerikeri that they were unable to see the folly of their proposals. The *Karere* cost £100 a year to run and had been built specifically for visits to distant tribes with a view to establishing new stations and obtaining of food supplies. Now she was to be out of commission while carrying stone for this useless store. Already she had been damaged by carrying stone to build William Williams' house at Paihia. They should build a punt if they wished to persist, for 'their knowledge of a vessel' he fumed 'does not exceed mine respecting a plough'. To Henry Williams' fulminations they protested they were building a punt, but needed the *Karere* too.

But it was all too late. The stonemason, Parrott, was already waiting in October 1831 to commence cutting stone, he, his wife and child having come from New South Wales on the ship which had brought back William Yate from another visit to that colony. Yate had been informed by the Corresponding Committee while in New South Wales that every possible means was to be used for the store's immediate commencement. Yate had also proposed at the October meeting 'that the plan presented by Mr Kemp of a store 50 feet by 30 two stories be adopted and that the work be commenced without further delay'. A small compromise had been made. With the *Karere* and Henry Williams still away, Parrott was to work on William Williams' 'half-built' stone house at Paihia. This house, the first stone building in New Zealand, later housed the mission's second printing press.

By April 1832 Parrott had faced the stone brought up from down the inlet. John Hobbs, that practical Wesleyan missionary friend, had drawn a working plan of the Stone Store and calculated the amount of timber needed which was to be cut at Styles and Harris timberyard at Hokianga. Mr Kinghorne, a mill builder, was coming to New Zealand to design a mill at Kerikeri. This was also to be of stone, and next to the Stone Store. On the spot where the store was to be, 500 bushels of lime had been made. Henry Williams could do no more than record his dissent to resolutions passed at the April 1832 meetings. The previous year's October resolutions were confirmed and it was agreed that Lewington, the skipper of the *Karere*, should get extra wages. James Kemp was to be relieved of his storeman's duties to oversee, with Charles Baker, the building of the Stone Store. Thomas Chapman was to be storekeeper. The mission ship *Active* was to be pressed into service to bring the timber around from the Hokianga Habour.

The foundation of the Stone Store was laid on 9 May 1832. Baker went in June to Hokianga to see to the loading of the plank on the *Active* — 36,230 feet for the store and 9,143 feet for the mill. George Clarke drew up an indent for quoins, jambs, archstones and steps which was sent off to Sydney in July, by which time Parrott had completed half the foundations.

The Kerikeri Station on 9 August 1841, sketched by Richard Taylor. To the left is a glimpse of the original store (1819). On the hill is the 1829 chapel and the former home of Charles Baker (1830). John Edmonds, the stonemason, had lived in the latter for a time but it was vacant and out of repair when the sketch was executed. By August 1841 only the Kemps were still at Kerikeri, living in the Mission House.
ALEXANDER TURNBULL LIBRARY

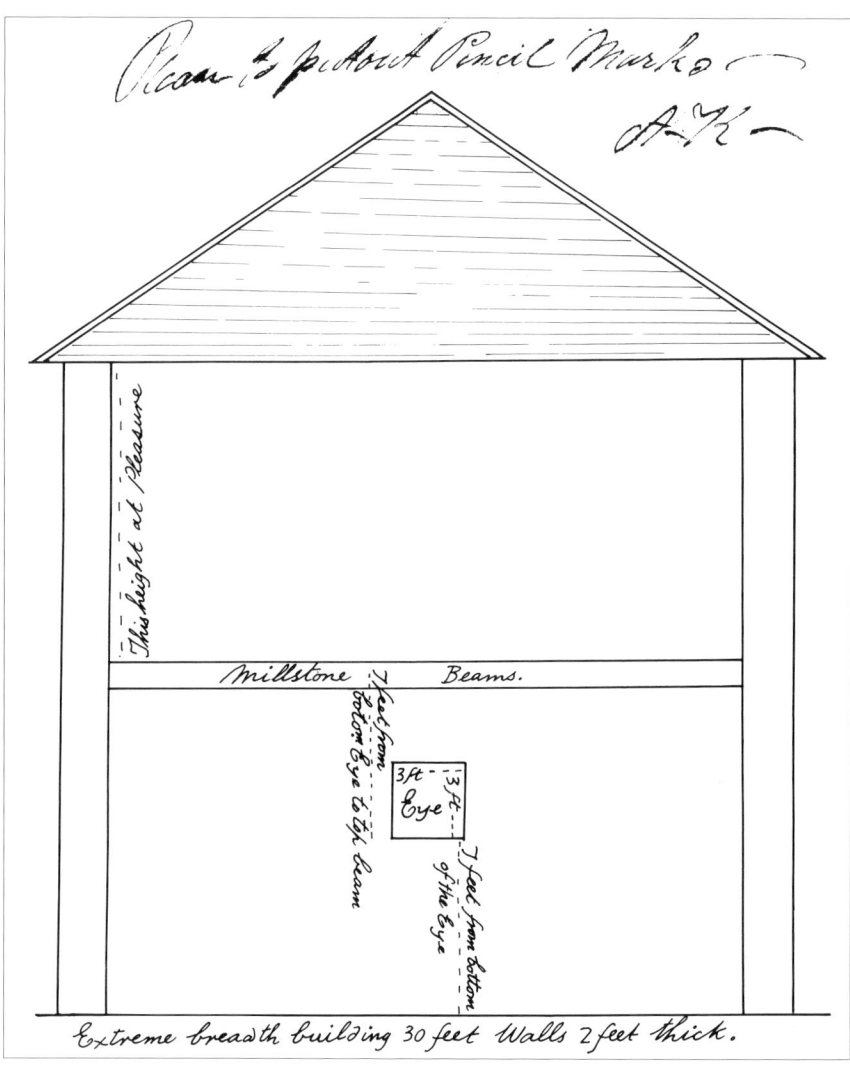

The stone millhouse designed by A. Kinghorne of New South Wales, which was to be built on the foreshore of the Kerikeri Basin. The design has been redrawn from the original in the papers of the Church Missionary Society
AUCKLAND PUBLIC LIBRARY

Kinghorne had been and gone, leaving a plan of the proposed mill race, the mill building and the mill works which he had designed to suit the site next to the store on the foreshore of the Kerikeri Basin. But after digging the foundations for the two buildings, the enthusiastic missionaries had qualms about the project. The Stone Store, Mill and Mission House could be in danger from the frequent flooding of the Kerikeri River through the millrace. Furthermore, because of the tidal rise in the Kerikeri Basin, the millwheel would not be able to turn for more than eight to ten hours a day. Kinghorne had evidently thought that the Wairoa Creek would be a better site. The land there had already been purchased for a native farm, and now they thought if the mill were built there it would afford the New Zealanders an equal opportunity for grinding their produce at this spot. The missionaries informed the Corresponding Committee that as soon as the mill house was built on the Wairoa they would send for the mill works. Hasty consultation by the Corresponding Committee with Kinghorne in New South Wales brought the reply that the design for the basin would not be suitable for the Wairoa. A new design would be needed and the expenditure would be too great to contemplate.

Marsden's seventeen-year old vision of a mill at Kerikeri was abandoned. Part of the plank earmarked for the mill was given to Baker who was expected to begin a mission at Kaitaia. Kinghorne's visit to New Zealand had been a costly waste of time and money — machinery for the mill and Kinghorne's expenses had been estimated at £240-£250. Fortunately the mill works were suitable for use in a mill at Bathurst, New South Wales, recouping some of the expense. A mill was begun the following year at the Waimate station, and at length, in 1834, the French burr millstones brought out in 1824 could be used to grind the mission wheat.

Under Parrott's skilled hands, assisted by native workmen, one of whom, Pawero, became a competent stonemason, the store's foundation of Kerikeri Inlet stone was finished by the end of September 1832. A stone cutting shed had been put up on the ground which had been levelled for a future stone wharf. In this shed Sydney sandstone which had come in January and July 1832 was being shaped. The stones which Clarke had drawn up arrived on the *Active* in October, a further source of anger for Henry Williams as the *Active* had to be redecked to transport the stone. A carpenter's shop for Nisbet the Scottish carpenter, and the forge for Kemp's blacksmithing for the store was put up by Nisbet behind the Mission House. It was probably about this time that the Butler's 1821 outhouse/kitchen was dismantled to make way for the new building. This building that, survived until the middle of this century, was known as the blacksmith's shop. Legend grew that it was the original blacksmith's shop built in 1819, but that shop, which stood near to the present tearooms, had gone by the late 1830s.

Parrott and his workmen had cut stone for a month or more and by January 1833 the walls were three feet high and ready for the sandstone window sills. Nisbet had been making fourteen window frames and preparing flooring. In June 1833 the Stone Store builders 'struck centre', the first shaped windowheads were put in and the arch over the doorway on which is engraved '1833' was fixed in place using the iron work made by James Kemp. Sixty more blocks of sandstone came on the *Active* in July, plenty for Parrott to go on cutting and cementing in as quoins in the Kerikeri Inlet basalt faces. Meanwhile Nisbet framed the roof and put in the joists of the first floor during the rest of 1833. By March 1834 Parrott's work was done — it had cost £173.1.3$^1/_2$ — and he and his wife and child took passage in the *Karere* to Whangaroa where he settled next to the former mission herdsman Spickman. The Stone Store shell of stone, with floor joists in place and roof framed and the chimney partly built, was ready to be finished by Nisbet and his workmen.

In the meantime, due to a misunderstanding between the Society in London and the Corresponding Committee in New South Wales, the stonemason, John Edmonds, was on his way to New Zealand. Arriving in Feburary 1834, with the stone work on the store all but finished, work had to be found for him. He was employed first on the Girls' School at Paihia, then at Kerikeri building a couple of chimneys on James Shepherd's house. Shepherd had replaced Chapman, who had gone to Paihia, as storekeeper in 1833 and was now in James Kemp's original 1820 house. And the Kerikeri-Waimate people expected that, apart from finishing the chimney and laying flagstones in the bottom half of the store, he would also be building a substantial stone wharf.

It is not clear when it was decided to raise the tower on the south-west corner of the store to house the settlement clock (which had been in the gable end of the chapel) and the large settlement bell. It was not part of the original plan, for the already framed roof was altered to construct the tower in May 1834. By October 1834 the 'belfry' with its venetian windows, the settlement clock in place, and a weathercock perched on the peak of its copper roof, was complete. The raising of the tower nearly had tragic consequences for Ben Nisbet when he fell twenty-three feet from the top of the store wall, but wrote Kemp . . . 'through mercy did not hurt himself he providentially lit on his feet.' He went on to complete the flooring, partitioning and lining of the store over the next two years, while the Maori workmen shingled the roof. Although the building had been declared by Shepherd late in 1835 to be finished and ready to receive the stores, in fact the staircase had not been built, the windows were unglazed, and the floor paving remained to be done. These were at last finished in the middle of 1836.

In the five years it had taken to build, the store had become the white elephant that Henry Williams had predicted it would. With the go ahead given for the opening up of southern stations it was more convenient to keep the stores handy to the shipping at the Bay and this was done from 1835 onwards. Still, the Kerikeri-Waimate people argued, it would be needed to house the flour ground at the Waimate mill which was expected from the 1836 harvest. What a quantity of flour it could accommodate — far more than the Waimate mill was capable of producing. In fact after 1836 this mill was producing less and less. Henry Williams was pressing for the closure of the Kerikeri Mission which he said was costing £800 a year to maintain. He said the store was a memorial to a waste of money and missionary purpose, but could perhaps be preserved, along with other buildings, to be used for invalids.

Nevertheless, Kerikeri still planned to have its stone wharf, and John Edmonds with a gang of Maori workmen embarked on the tremendous task of cutting a road from the store through the hill to join with the road to Waimate, to allow the bullocky Peleg Wood to bring his waggon from Waimate right down to the store. At that time goods had to be manhandled up or down a steep path to be loaded on to or unloaded from the waggon. Road cutting was Edmond's chief employment for over a year until March 1838, by which time the hill had been cut down twelve feet over a distance of 300 yards. He also began to collect more stone from down the Inlet to build a temporary wharf. This was built by Edmonds in the first half of 1839 and the remains of the stonework of this pier, can still be seen under the present wharf. This was to be his last building task at Kerikeri. As his services were no longer required, a plan for a stone printing shop at Waimate having been abandoned, he built a stone house on his farm down the Inlet. Although his connection with the Society was severed, he was to return to Kerikeri and the Stone Store over twenty years later.

James Kemp, with the store completed, once more took over the management of the stores from James Shepherd who had removed to Whangaroa. He was helped by his son James Kemp Jnr. One of James Kemp's sons would eventually buy the Stone Store which was described by Lady Franklin in 1841 as the 'best built structure I have seen in New Zealand', a tribute to the workmanship of Parrott, Nisbet, Kemp, Edmonds and the Maori carpenters and stonecutters.

The suggestion that the Stone Store might be used as a Native School was made by both Kemp and Henry Williams. This idea might have been acted on had not Bishop Selwyn arrived in 1842 carrying with him a letter of instruction from the Society to the New Zealand missionaries. The

Bishop, they wrote, would need a place at his command in which he could safely place his valuable library and, 'the Commee had much pleasure in offering to receive it into the Society's Store at Kerikeri for any length of time he might require.' Selwyn was the first Missionary Bishop sent out by the Church of England to the colonies and gloried in that character. An ecclesiastical library was essential to his calling, and friends and colleagues in England had endowed him with a bountiful supply of books which would be the basis of a library for the new Diocese of New Zealand. In a land of wood-clad and shingled buildings, the Stone Store was a remarkable structure, evoking for Selwyn nostalgic memories of his happy years as a chaplain at Powis Castle. The massive stone walls may not have equalled in thickness those of Powis Castle but accorded well, he said, 'with the solid and venerable character of the contents of the library . . .' 'Certainly George was as happy as a king here . . .' Mrs Selwyn was to record.

But these remarks were made over a year after the Bishop had arrived. As he found, there was much work to be done before his books were on Nisbet's shelves in an upper room. While the Bishop set off almost immediately on an extended journey around his large diocese, furniture (including Sarah Selwyn's piano) and the cases of books were brought up to the Stone Store. James Kemp was kept busy over six months with the 'necessary attention to be paid to his Lordship' and in being 'occupied with the Lord Bishop's Public Library'. Not all the books could fit on Nisbet's dusted off shelves and new shelves were to be made to form a free

Before coming to New Zealand, Bishop Selwyn had served as chaplain in Powis Castle. The thick stone walls of the Stone Store reminded Selwyn of his former residence. This sketch of Powis Castle was made from a photograph.

standing wall which would screen a bed and washstand for the Bishop or his Chaplain's convenience when they came from Waimate (where the Bishop was establishing his St John's College) for 'two or three days hard reading'. It was hard walking, too, as the Chaplain William Cotton ruefully reflected on Bishop Selwyn's words to him as he trudged back the ten miles from Kerikeri to Waimate nursing a sore knee: 'We shall be ashamed' the Bishop had said, 'to go so far and do nothing'.

The Society agent, Sampson Kempthorne, was working to secure a lease for Selwyn of the Stone Store and the wharf for seven years at £100 a year. Selwyn's occupation would require disposing of the stores which remained there. 'It is almost incredible' Kempthorne wrote in his report, 'the quantity of useless stores, lumber, old iron pots, tools etc. etc. which are here and at many other stations. There is an old secondhand fire engine here, now rotten, which has never been used.' Selwyn planned for the Stone Store to be the 'Grange' to Waimate. He and Mrs Selwyn would use three of the rooms as a 'retreat'. The other space, apart from the library, would be filled 'with the appurtenances of Churches, windows, doors and ornamental work of every kind in stone and wood, Fonts, Pulpits, Lecterns, Seats . . .' Working models would come from the Cambridge Camden Society and the Maori, whose ingenuity in carving was well known, would convert stone and wood to churches to the Glory of God in the Norman style. This style, he commented, was appropriate being the style of the first churches in England. As well, 'its rudeness and massiveness . . . [would] probably render it easier to be understood and appreciated by them . . .' Norman style churches could be built throughout the country ornamented along the top of the walls with the 'grotesques' which he seemed to think were akin to Maori carved figures. Had his inspiration been put into practice Norman replicas in stone would have been seen instead of the distinctive wooden 'Selwyn' churches which we treasure today.

In their old age, the Bishop envisioned Mrs Selwyn and himself retiring to live in the 'beautiful stone building'. His hopeful projections for the use of the store were not realised except for the library room and the one immediately below it. The Northern District Missionary Committee voted to dispose of the 'useless stores' spoken of by Kempthorne, to two of Kemp's sons who agreed to pay £300 down on 3 August 1843 and a further £150 over 18 months. The stores remained to litter the building when Selwyn sat in the library room with his wife, William Cotton and Mrs Burrows in October 1843, waiting for the wind to abate so that they might sail to Auckland. 'The charm of this library' he wrote to the Rev. E. Coleridge,

is that it is so utterly uncolonial . . . Its walls are worthy of a college, My books

> *carry me back to the first ages of the Church. It is true when I step outside the door I stumble over a mass of utilitarian treasures. Bales of blankets, iron pots, barrels of all kinds, rusty rat-traps and saws, old chains, grindstones etc, are the miscellaneous furniture of my ante-chambers; but within everything that can most elevate and purify the mind is to be found.*

The quiet companions sat reading or writing, Cotton sitting on a box on one side of the fireplace, Mrs Selwyn on the other upon a broken backed chair reading from a volume placed on Selwyn's desk. A pile of planks intended for the extra bookshelves and resting on bullockhide trunks made a seat for the Bishop and Mrs Burrows.

When the Selwyns returned through Kerikeri to Waimate in the summer of 1844 the library had been lined with timber by Peleg Wood. 'It was quite necessary to do so' wrote Mrs Selwyn to a friend

> *as the Mortar was so bad and crumbling, that the books were being injured by the dust; but the planed wood is a bad substitute for the massive stone walls, and the wooden ceiling is very ugly. Nevertheless it is by far the nicest room still in NZ.*

The Bishop thought so too, writing

> *A delicious day in my library. Books all arranged around me. Such a sight is not to be seen in New Zealand so refreshing and inspiriting. I now purpose to devote a day and a half every week to quiet reading.*

The new bookshelves were in place on the west wall, a table had been made for the room and there was a sofa, but even with these improvements some books were piled on the floor.

The room beneath the library, one of those for a 'retreat' for Mrs Selwyn, seems not to have been used by her, as she stayed with the Kemps in the Mission House when at Kerikeri. But in July 1844 the Bambridges came down from Waimate for a few days' break, to find that the Bishop had cleared the room and had ready prepared for them a beautiful dinner of potted beef and soup. He acted as a waiter to Sophia Bambridge while she ate. Young Mr Fisher from Waimate was there also. A three legged iron pot stood over the fire in the fireplace. Bambridge noted that

> *Mr Fisher thought the Bishop wanted it to boil quickly, so began to blow it very considerably and in a few minutes the wooden foundation [the firewood] gave way when the contents of the pot were extended over the nice clean room. Poor Mr Fisher's phiz and the floor looked in a sorry condition.*

The floor of Sydney sandstone probably absorbed the water fairly readily. These flags are now covered by timber flooring. As a result of this accident

Stone Store and Mill

Above: *The Episcopal Work 'us'. This ink sketch by T.B. Hutton was, according to William Cotton, 'faithful down to the Bishop's umbrella lying upon the table'. Many of the books listed here, and Bishop Selwyn's desk, are now in St John's College, Auckland. The sketch is from the W.C. Cotton Journal.*
DIXSON LIBRARY, SYDNEY
Left: *The fireplace in the room beneath Bishop Selwyn's library in the*

continued on page 138

continued from page 137

Stone Store, was sketched by William Bambridge, when he, his wife Sophia and son Willy stayed there in July 1844. On the fire is the 'new American oven'. 'We cooked some pork and potatoes excellently' wrote Bambridge, in his diary, 'but I think it is an article suited only to those who have plenty of servants at command.
ALEXANDER TURNBULL LIBRARY

Selwyn tried out his new American oven on the fire. 'We cooked pork and potatoes excellently', wrote Bambridge, 'but I think it is an article suited only to those who have plenty of servants at command . . . to clean up things.'

Only a few months after this happy holiday at Kerikeri, Selwyn and his colleagues were on their way to Auckland to transfer St John's College to land above the Purewa Creek at Meadowbank. In October 1844 the cherished volumes, inscribed by friends from Magdalene College, Oxford, from Eton, from Cambridge University, from many ministers and authors of religious works — all these went into boxes, including the Selwyn Family Bible bearing the signature of young Willy Selwyn's famous godfather, W.E. Gladstone. Another bible which opened at its inscription 'To the Lord Bishop of New Zealand with the best wishes of his Affectionate Pupils at Powis Castle' perhaps in the future brought to the Selwyns' mind the Stone Store and the loved library room there.

With Selwyn gone from Kerikeri the Stone Store was once more in the care of James Kemp. Scarcely more than six months after Selwyn and his entourage had departed, the building was packed with troops soaked to the skin on their way to do battle with Heke and Kawiti's forces. The store became a magazine during the months of June-September when the British troops fought the futile battle of Ohaeawai. When the dust of battle had settled, trading began again in the store. James' son, Richard Kemp, recorded in the period up to 1857 much trade with European settlers who had flocked to the Bay from the late 1830s. Many Maori who bought goods at the store worked off their debt in labour putting up fences on the Kemp farmlands, shearing sheep and splitting shingles. Kauri gum, which was also traded at the store, was thought at first to be a great blessing to the Maori as a supplement to their income from wheat growing. It was to turn sour later when the Maori, driven by poverty, dispersed all over the north to dig gum, even on Sundays to the dismay of the Church people, who blamed the government. The outstanding debt on the stores bought in 1843 from the Society by Kemp's sons was released to their father James in 1852 as full and final settlement on his termination of employment with the Society in 1850.

There were, however, two articles in the Stone Store which were still the Society's property — the fire engine and the bell in the tower. The clock had been removed to the renovated second church at Waimate early in 1844. The bell, cast in 1815, the year of the Battle of Waterloo, may have been the bell sent out to Thomas Kendall in 1822. This bell, the first church bell in New Zealand, was brought to Kerikeri in 1823 following Kendall's dismissal. Taken down from the belfry of the Stone Store in 1851, it was shipped to the Rev. R. Maunsell's station at Waikato Heads,

A box 'well nailed together serving the very useful purpose of conveying Mr Kemp's firewood from the opposite shore' was a boat for 'D[ea]r Soph and Willy' in July 1844 wrote William Bambridge in his diary, from which this sketch is taken.
ALEXANDER TURNBULL LIBRARY

then up river to Maunsell's second station at Te Kohanga. The bell hung there by the church until it was boated across the Waikato River to the comparative safety of Waiuku when the Te Kohanga Mission Station became derelict following the Land Wars. There at Holy Trinity Church a stout frame of Awhitu totara supported its 419 lbs until 1913 when it was returned by the Anglican Church to the Te Kohanga Maori. Today this old bell hangs from an iron tower next to the small church on Te Kotahitanga Marae above the Waikato River. The fire engine, which should have been sent to Waimate in 1838, and was possibly unassembled and still in numbered packages, was sent to St Stephens College in Parnell, from where it was to be sold.

The problem of what to do with the large, unprofitable Stone Store building kept cropping up for the New Zealand branch of the Society, which was by now in charge of the maintenance of buildings. In 1848 it had been suggested that 'settlers' be invited to form a committee to manage the store and the Society's mill at Waimate. Nothing seems to have come of this and the store was probably leased to Richard Kemp under a yearly 'repairing' lease scheme. At the beginning of 1857, however, a more regular agreement was drawn up between the Society and Ebenezer Norris for a three year lease of the Stone Store and wharf at £35 a year. Norris married Charlotte Kemp in 1859 and renewed the lease on the store for a further four years, along with the land on which the original 1819-20 buildings had stood. Norris had lived for a time in all that remained of James Kemp's 1820 house, the stone walled kitchen added in 1831. But in 1860 he built a cottage on his leased land where the present tearooms now stand. In 1864 Norris relinquished his lease and the Stone Store was empty.

The next proposal for its use was as an 'industrious school' — a Native District School where Maori pupils would board while learning a trade. The Colonial Secretary declined the Church Missionary Society's offer and the store was leased to another Kemp son, James Kemp Jnr. Kemp Jnr sublet it to John Edmonds, the former stonemason, who purchased the goods in the store. John Edmonds, recently married for a second time, was to have a short tenure as storekeeper. In July 1865, a year after taking over, he was dead 'of a carbuncle'. Who was storekeeper after this is not known, but by early 1867 the Stone Store had a scandalous reputation, being known as the Church Missionary grog shop. The doors of the grog shop were hastily closed by the committee and James Kemp Jnr bought back the stores from John Edmonds' son Samuel. James Jnr still had a number of years to run on his fourteen year lease and was hoping to get the approval of the Society committee to run a school in part of it. For the third time its proposed use as a school came to nothing. James Kemp's rent, which had been £66 per annum in 1867 was first reduced to £40 and finally to £36 in 1870. In this year he informed the committee that the store roof was leaking badly. At this time fixed skylights which had replaced the dormer windows some time after 1858 were repaired and hinged.

Permission was finally given to sell the Stone Store which had been a burden to the Society since it was first proposed. In January 1874 James Kemp Jnr purchased it for £500, although he was not to get title to the property for almost twenty years. Storekeeping does not appear to have been very profitable, for in 1891 he still owed £200 and arrears of interest. By 1892 he had cleared his debt, the Society magnanimously waiving £50 of the originally agreed purchase price. In 1893, for £450 and a considerable amount of interest paid over the years, James Kemp Jnr at last had the title deeds in his hands.

In 1888 he had thankfully handed over the storekeeping to the American John Black. To his son Frank he wrote.

> *I feel very much better for leaving the Store, and I am sure I should have injured my health if I had persisted in keeping it on. A Mr Black has it now is very energetic and I think so far pleased with his prospects.*

John Black's prospects included marriage to Kemp's daughter, Ethel Jane. During Black's time as storekeeper there was a great trade in kauri gum which lay in aromatic heaps on the first floor of the store, where it was sorted and graded from the beautiful clear amber of the best grade, down to the chalky lowest grade.

At some point the troublesome shingle roof was replaced with corrugated iron, possibly as late as 1910. The original chimney had disappeared before 1888, a number of Maori helping to pull it down.

> *A long strong rope was attached to the chimney and the Maoris commenced to pull. But the old mortar was stronger than had been supposed, and the chimney resisted all efforts to bring it down. Suddenly the rope broke and amid great laughter the long line of Maoris went down. . . . When all had recovered from their mirth and enjoyment a further effort with a stronger rope was made, and this time the chimney was brought down safely.*

Shorn of its attractive dormers, chimney and belfry and with its ugly skylighted iron roof, the Stone Store remained this way until it was bought in 1976 by the Historic Places Trust. In September 1990 a brick chimney, reinstalled a few years earlier, had (due to unforeseen effects on the Stone Store structure) to be 'brought down' once more. However, with the restored dormers and the roof once more shingled, much of the exterior charm of this, the earliest remaining stone building in New Zealand, has been regained.

Stone Store and Mill

The Kerikeri Mission Station in 1869. The house to the left of the picture was built by E.G. Norris in 1859, on the site of the 1819 buildings. Norris leased the Stone Store from 1857 to 1863. This picture is taken from the Illustrated New Zealand Herald, *22 December 1869.*
HOCKEN LIBRARY, DUNEDIN

John Kinder photographed the Waianiwaniwa Falls, under the title of 'Kerikeri Falls', some time in the 1860s.
AUCKLAND INSTITUTE AND MUSEUM

Section 4

The Wharepoke and Waianiwaniwa Falls

John Liddiard Nicholas journeyed with Marsden through Kerikeri in January 1815. 'The river' wrote Nicholas, 'that discharged itself into the cove, was called by the natives Tecaddiecaddie . . . its banks in many parts were lined with timber, which the natives float down the stream as occasion requires. A little way from its mouth is a fall that might with no great trouble be made strong enough to turn machinery'. These falls were known in the early years of the mission as the Kerikeri Falls. The name Wharepoke was in fact that of the small wood to the north side of the falls. It was from this wood, the only stand of timber near to the mission station, that logs were split for the paling fences enclosing the houses of the first settlers.

Members of the Duperrey expedition visited the station in 1824. The French medical man Lesson, writing of diseases of the New Zealanders, observed that they were sometimes overcome with cramps which they named 'Keke' and with 'gravelle' which they called 'Kiddi-Kiddi' a word, he said, which signified also, a cascade or water chute. The 'Cascade' (the Kerikeri Falls) and the wood 'Warree puke' they marked on their map.

Samuel Stutchbury, a visiting zoologist with the Pacific Pearl Fishing Co., wrote in his journal of 1826 'Before dinner we walked to the waterfall from which the River derives its name . . . its approach to the perpendicular was thro' a vale over a black basaltic bottom . . . running with a most transparent glassiness, and suddenly arriving at the fall plunges down the Abyss, where it continues rushing over loose fragments of the Rock with sullen roar'.

The missionaries Charles Baker, James Hamlin and William Yate all wrote of the wood 'Warepuke'. From this wood Yate lifted young native trees to plant in his garden at the mission. And it was to this shaded place of bush and water that the missionary families and the New Zealanders living with them, sometimes went on Christmas Day. One afternoon on Christmas Day 1830 'we with our families had a walk and took tea in the bush' wrote Charles Baker; and William Yate also noting this Christmas picnic at 'Ware Puke' wrote of gifts of pipes and tobacco being given that day to the mission Maori.

The first buildings (1819–20) had sagged on their rotting foundations within a very few years. James Hamlin, enquiring from the Maori, learned that the puriri tree, (sometimes called the 'New Zealand Oak' for its hardness, or New Zealand cherry from its profusion of rosy berries) was 'so durable that it will scarcely ever rot'. Ground plates of this tough wood from the Wharepoke bush were used as foundations for the second chapel at Kerikeri, built on the hill. Puriri groves were often tapu to the Maori, sacred places where their dead rested for a time, and where tapu articles associated with sacred rites were placed. In mission times there is no suggestion whatever of Wharepoke being such a place.

Kauri logs felled at Papakauri in 1829 were floated down to the waterfall, where they were cut on the spot for laths for William Yate's lath and plaster house then being built. It is said that in this century, there was still an iron ring in the rock near the fall to which kauri logs had been tied. These were the falls whose power was to be harnessed by the mill planned for Kerikeri, but never built, which is discussed in the preceeding section.

By the 1930s the Kerikeri Falls had acquired the name Wharepoke. Today the path to the falls is signposted above the Stone Store. At the falls, the bush to the north still shades the water, while on the south side the path approaches the falls through a mixture of exotic and native trees, leading to a viewing platform above the pool. Had Kinghorne's 1832 mill race been built, the path might instead have traced another route, beside channel and flume from the top of the falls to a mill wheel on the shore of the Kerikeri Basin.

The beauty of the Waianiwaniwa Falls, the Waters of the Rainbow, has been celebrated by artists and writers since the Kerikeri Mission Station was founded in 1819. Every visitor to Kerikeri seems to have been taken to see them. To reach the falls much the same route was taken as the one followed by travellers in cars today. There was no bridge across the Kerikeri River then of course, (the first was built in 1913) and visitors were put across the water from the Mission Station by boat to climb up to the high ground where they followed an old Maori track.

One hot summer's day in 1825, Marianne Williams and others at the settlement set off to the falls, taking she wrote,

> *some bottles of porter and milk for our refreshment. Mr Kemp after putting us across the river in his boat stayed in charge of the settlement. The native paths through the fern admit of only one person walking at a time, so that we formed a long train as the road wound over the hills.*

The Waterfalls 147

The falls were screened by forest at the approach, and although the muffled roar of the waters was heard, it was not until they broke through the encircling bush on to the rocky shore of the basin, that the grandeur of the fall was revealed.

The track which the rangers of the Bay of Islands Maritime and Historic Park Board have made takes a different route, but arriving at the same place, these spectacular falls have the same impact. Beginning by the Ranger Station, the modern track soon leads into quiet bush by massy rock bluffs, then down to a pretty valley alongside the Kerikeri River. Wooden walkways carry the track across one or two swampy watercourses running into the river. Through here an early visitor was misled by a 'sharp little urchin' of a guide, 'who contrived to lead us into five or six bogs where we were up to our knees in water'.

The level path wanders through a totara grove at a turn in the river where the Kerikeri is joined by the Puketotara Stream on the opposite side. From up this stream timber cut by missionaries in the late 1820s was floated down to the Mission Station, part of it being used in building the second (1829) chapel. Just above the confluence on the far side was, in

This early depiction of the Waianiwaniwa Falls is based on a sketch by Jules Le Jeune done in 1824. His sketch was later used as the basis for a handcoloured engraving and aquatint. The picture was titled 'Cascade de Fanafaoua pres du village de Kidikidi'.
ALEXANDER TURNBULL LIBRARY

1824, the Maori village of 200 whare, 'Poukarra Karra'. A short distance on, the falls burst upon the view much as they did for the first visitors, one of whom wrote this charming description:

> *the water of the river . . . falls at once down a perpindicular descent of variously coloured rock . . . into a lovely sequestered basin, from which the river flows through a wooded ravine, in perfect contrast to the extensive barreness of the surrounding country. The mist raised by the dashing of the waters displays in sunshine a partial rainbow . . . Behind the fall is a large cave before which the falling water forms a glittering, transparent ever-moving curtain.*

This cave has its tale of olden times. In the days when the Ngati Rehia tribe had all the land about Kerikeri, the Hokianga tribes came against them. The Ngati Rehia warriors, defeated in battle and making their way home, were met by the kaumatua of their tribe by a waterfall on the Puketotara River. The kaumatua rallied them with the cry 'Whakahoki. Kei a matou te Kaha' — 'Turn back. The strength is in the old ones'. Hence the name Whakahoki was given to those falls where, inspired by this call, the warriors turned back with their old men, scattering the pursuing Hokianga, a large number of whom hid in the cave beneath the Waianiwaniwa Falls. But they were found, killed and eaten there by the triumphant Ngati Rehia.

The cave was said to be a favourite place of the Colonial Botanist, Alan Cunningham, who first explored its profuse plant life in 1826, sending a number of specimens of ferns and other plants to Kew Gardens, London. In later times (1844) a party of schoolboys (and five dogs) in the charge of Rev. W.C. Cotton crashed their way one drizzly day down an overgrown track from Waimate to enjoy a birthday picnic at the falls. They also took refuge in the cave, but this time to light a 'glorious' fire and cook their potatoes.

The placid basin below the falls had been the scene of great activity in June 1821. Kauri logs felled in February at the Kahikatearoa forest, some distance upstream from the falls, had been rolled into the water. When the winter rains swelled the river, the men of the settlement and the New Zealanders went to Kahikatearoa. 'The natives with very manly courage, threw off every article of clothing, and rushed into the rapid current and released the logs from their lodgments'. Thirty-two logs were got over the falls that day. Once in the basin below 'the eddy was so strong that it was with the utmost difficulty we got them from under the fall. Mr F. Hall was once in the water over head, and narrowly escaped the loss of his life.' Almost all the logs were, by nightfall, got into the mainstream where the river, its course previously cleared of obstacles, carried them down to within 'a short distance' of the mission settlement.

An easy, short climb up the track from the bottom of the falls brings you out on to a grassed and shrub planted area, and to another path which leads to three viewing platforms. One overhangs the cliff encircling the basin, much closer to the falling torrent at this higher level, while down below is the deep basin and the thicket of trees which clothe the steep slopes. The other platforms, reached a little further on, are closer to the top of the falls. Here, one can imagine Edward Markham in 1834 being 'pikaued' across to the opposite bank.

> *I crossed over on a Man's shoulders, he leaping from Stone to Stone and in the middle my Hat blew off. I caught it but the Native tried to catch a pair of Cotton gloves. That had nearly been fatal to both, as he slipped from the stone but sprang forward and recovered himself.*

Kemp turned faint at the sight, and Markham's treasured little dog, Venus, who had followed them halfway across sat down and whined. Rescued by the Maori, she was passed safely to her master on the far side.

A tramway crossed above these falls in 1909, when timber felled in the Puketi Forest was hauled by steam engine down to the Waipapa landing, a few miles down the inlet from Kerikeri. Beside the path near the falls, and running under it, is a ditch, which was dug in 1930, a race to channel water to power the turbine of the generator which gave electricity to the new settlers at Kerikeri — the citrus growers. Through their efforts Kerikeri was the first place north of Whangarei to have electricity.

Although it has been written many times that the Rev. Samuel Marsden was the first mission visitor to see the falls in 1815, this is not so. When Marsden's Journal was edited, a reference to the nine foot fall at Kerikeri was mistakenly read as ninety feet, and the assumption made that he had seen the Waianiwaniwa Falls. In fact, Frances Hall and James Kemp were the first to venture there in 1822. There have been some notable visitors to the Waianiwaniwa Falls, including the above mentioned Colonial Botanist, Alan Cunningham, Thomas Henry Huxley, biologist, with Capt. Owen Stanley of the *Rattlesnake*, and Sir James Clark Ross, stopping in the Bay of Islands on his way to explore Antarctic waters in 1841. With Ross on the *Erebus* was the botanist Sir Joseph Dalton Hooker, who was later famous as the Director of Kew Gardens. Sir James found the appearance of the falls

> *very striking, the rapid stream which the eye may trace winding several miles along the extensive plain, precipitates a broad sheet of water over an escarpment of black basaltic columns about seventy feet high into a deep circular basin whose shores are thickly wooded.*

Today this 'extensive plain' is farmed or covered with orchards, and trees obscure the landscape, but in minutes by car or in an hour or so on foot from the Kerikeri Basin modern visitors too can delight in the Waters of the Rainbow.

Bishop Selwyn had jokingly anticipated (in 1843) the day 'when Tea Gardens will flourish, and a board with Guide to the Falls makes its appearance over the door of young Mr Kemp.' On the site of the original buildings at Kerikeri, there now stands a tearoom with a broad verandah overlooking the peaceful basin with its moored yachts.

Appendix 1

Chronology 1819–1874

1819
- August: Church Missionary Society carpenters Bean and Fairburn at Kerikeri to erect the blacksmith's shop (erected September) the first permanent building in Kerikeri.
Second building erected to house Maori workmen.
- October: Third Building — the Storehouse.
- December: The families come from Rangihoua to Kerikeri. James Kemp and wife and Francis Hall occupy the blacksmith's shop. Storehouse is quarters for Rev. J. Butler, Bean, Fairburn, Puckey and families.

1820
- February: James Kemp's and Francis Hall's house begun.
- March: Hongi Hika leaves with Thomas Kendall for England.
- April/May: Butler's Mission House, (now Kemp House) garden laid out.
- November: Marsden, Butler, Shepherd, Puckey go to Waitemata Harbour.
- December: Kitchen/outhouse to Mission House begun.

1821
- June: Mission House begun.
- July: Hongi Hika returns from England.
- September: War parties leave Kerikeri.
- November: Butler and family move into outhouse/kitchen of Mission House. Butler goes to New South Wales.
- December: War parties return from southern raids.

1822
- February: War parties set off again.
Butler returns from New South Wales.
- March: Butler moves into Mission House.

	May:	Bean, Fairburn and families return to New South Wales.
	July:	War parties return.
	December:	Francis Hall returns to England.

1823

	February:	War parties leave.
	June:	Butler and Shepherd accompany Wesleyans to found their mission at Whangaroa.
	August:	Marsden arrives from New South Wales with Rev. H. Williams and family. Fairburn and family return.
	November:	Butler suspended. He and family leave with Marsden for New South Wales.
		Henry Williams and family at Paihia.
	December:	Hongi's European style house on Kororipo Point begun by Puckeys.
		First Chapel being built.

1824

	April:	Clarke family arrive with the Duperrey expedition.
	August:	Davis family come to Kerikeri. Share Mission House with Clarkes. Also Charles Davis (no relation) to Kerikeri.
	December:	Shepherd leaves Kerikeri.

1825

	May:	Charles, son of Hongi Hika, killed at Kaipara.
	December:	Hongi goes to Kaipara to fight.

1826

	March:	James Hamlin and wife arrive Kerikeri.
		Rewa overcomes the Paroa Tribe (South-west Bay of Islands.)
	December:	Hongi goes to Whangaroa.

1827

	March:	Hongi severely wounded in tribal battle. Whangaroa mission destroyed. Refugees come to Kerikeri and go on to Paihia.
	June:	Hongi leaves Waimate and Kerikeri for good.

1828

	January:	Bridge built across Waitotorongo Creek.
		Rev. William Yate comes to Kerikeri.
	March:	Hongi Hika dies.
	June:	Charles Baker and family arrive at Kerikeri.

1829

	September:	Hongi's European house burns down.
	November:	Building of Chapel on hill begun.

Chronology

1830
  August: First printing press at Kerikeri.
                  Plans to establish inland station at Waimate.

1831
  January: Yate, Clarke, Hamlin, Davis, go to Waimate.
  March: 'Childrens Land' at Kerikeri purchased.
                  Chapman and wife to Kerikeri.
  May: Foundation of Stone Store laid.

1832
  July: Kemp Family move into Mission House.

1833
  June: Shepherd to Kerikeri, Chapman to Paihia.

1834
  February: John Edmonds and family arrive Bay of Islands. Come to Kerikeri in May.

1836
  July: Stone Store finished.

1839
  June: Shepherd and family go to Whangaroa.
                Edmonds family have left Kerikeri to farm down inlet.
                Kemps alone remain at Kerikeri.

1842
  June: Bishop Selwyn arrives to establish St. John's College at Waimate. Uses Stone Store for housing his library.

1844
  December: Selwyn leaves Bay of Islands.

1845
  May: War in the North. Military and marines occupy mission buildings on way to fight inland.

1860
                James Kemp owns Mission House (Kemp House).

1874
                Stone Store sold to James Kemp Jr.

Appendix 2

Cast

Maori Chiefs who frequented Kerikeri in early mission times and are mentioned in the text.

Hongi Hika	Hihi
Rewa (Manu)	Wharepoaka
Moka	Hone Heke
Tareha	'Towee'
Pakira	Titore
Wharerahi	Tinana

Missionary men and employees resident at Kerikeri and mentioned in the text, up until 1834, giving the year of arrival and occupation on arrival.

1819   *Missionaries*
Rev. John Gare Butler (New Zealands first resident clergyman; see Appendix 3)
Samuel Butler (Son of above)
Francis Hall (Schoolmaster)
James Kemp (Blacksmith)
James Shepherd, (At Okura for part of 1820)
Employees
William Fairburn (Carpenter, later missionary)
William Bean (Carpenter)
William Puckey (Carpenter, former ship's captain)
William Puckey Jnr. (Became carpenter, later a mission schoolmaster)
Richard Russell (Servant to Butler)
James Boyle (Saltman)

Cast

1821 *Missionary*
James Shepherd (Return to New Zealand as missionary settler)
Employee
John Lee (Husbandman)

1824 *Missionaries*
George Clarke (Schoolmaster)
Charles Davis (Schoolmaster)
Richard Davis (Farmer)
Employee
William Spickman (Herdsman)

1826 *Missionary*
James Hamlin (Flax dresser and weaver)

1828 *Missionaries*
Rev. William Yate
Charles Baker (Nurseryman)

1830 *Missionary*
Thomas Chapman (Storekeeper)
Employee
James Nisbet (Carpenter)

1831 *Employee*
William Parrott (Stonesmason)

1834 *Missionary*
John Edmonds (Stonemason)

Note: The wives of missionaries were also considered by the Church Missionary Society to be missionaries.

Appendix 3

John Gare Butler

John Gare Butler was said by his great-grandson R.J. Barton to have been born in March 1781. Baptismal records of the Parish of Stowe IX Churches in Northhamptonshire show him to have been baptised on 14 April 1782. In the village of Stowe, where his father was a labourer, Butler was educated at the Sunday School. He later worked for the local clergyman, the Rev. Charles Crawley, in his garden. As a youth he joined a brother in London, marrying a Miss Hitchman in 1798 at the early age of sixteen or seventeen. Their firstborn, Samuel died in infancy. Their second son, also named Samuel, was born in December 1800. In September 1817 a daughter Hannah was born. These children were named for John Butler's parents. During his twenty years in London he worked first as a clerk and then as a book keeper to a boat company at Paddington. Children of workers on the Paddington Canal attended a Sunday School run by the Rev. John Bishop whom John Butler assisted. At the age of thirty-five or thirty-six John Butler and his son Samuel (then seventeen) were accepted by the Church Missionary Society as missionary candidates. This was in June 1817. John Gare Butler was ordained Deacon on 19 September 1818 at Wells. Ordination as priest by the Bishop of Gloucester followed on 15 November 1818, by which time a decision of the Church Missionary Society had altered his destination from Sierra Leone to New Zealand. Clergymen such as John Butler were ordained specifically for missionary work on 'the credit of the Society without Title.' That is, lacking the educational background of Church of England ministers they were expected not to return to England nor have any pecuniary claim on the Church of England authorities should they do so. John Butler, his wife and children (Hannah, aged two, and Samuel, eighteen) left London in December 1818, arriving at the Bay of Islands, via Sydney, on 12 August 1819. He remained at Kerikeri for almost three years. Back in England by January 1825, he resigned from the Society's service. He found various positions as a curate in England until, in April 1840, he was once more, with his daughter, in New Zealand, this time at Petone as a clergyman ministering to the New Zealand Company settlers. Here he died on 18 June 1841 at the age of fifty-nine or sixty.

Glossary

Ariki	First-born male or female in a family of note; a leader
Atua	God, supernatural being, demon, ghost
Aute	Paper mulberry
Hakari	Entertainment, feast; the high wooden framework on which food was placed at a feast
Hapu	Section of a large tribe, clan, secondary tribe
Hue	Gourd
Karakia	Charm, spell, incantation
Kaumatua	Adult, old man or woman
Kumara	Sweet potato
Mana	Authority, control, influence, prestige, power; psychic force
Maori	Normal, usual, ordinary; now a person of the indigenous race of New Zealand
Mere	A short flat weapon of stone, for hand-to-hand fighting
Moko	Tattoo
Muru	Plunder
Pa	Stockade, fortified place
Pakeha	Person of predominantly European descent
Pakepakeha	Imaginary beings, resembling people, with fair skins
Rahui	A mark to warn people against trespassing; used in cases of tapu or for temporary protection of fruit, birds, fish etc.
Rangatira	Chief, male or female; well-born, noble; person of good breeding
Raupo	Bulrush
Rongo Pai	Good News
Take	Cause, reason; root or stump

Tapu	Under religious or superstitious restriction
Tangihanga	A weeping or mourning over
Taua	Hostile expedition
Teretere	Company of travellers
Taro	A root plant cultivated for food
Tangata Whenua	The people of the land; the original inhabitants
Tupuna (Tipuna)	Ancestor, grandparent
Umu	Earth oven
Utu	Return for anything; satisfaction, ransom, reward, price, reply
Waiata	Song
Wairua	Spirit
Waka	Canoe
Wakanui	Great canoe
Wakataua	War canoe
Whakapapa	Genealogical table; line of descent
Wharekarakia	A house or room for prayer

N.B. For technical reasons the macron denoting the long 'a' sound in Maori words is not used in this book.

Index

Aotearoa (New Zealand) 15

Baker, Rev. Charles Baker 68-9, 78, 80-1, 84, 123, 129, 131, 145-6
Baker, Mrs Hannah 68-9
Bambridge, Rev. William 124, 136, 138
Bambridge, Mrs Sophia 136
Bay of Islands Maritime and Historic Park Board 12, 147
Bean, William 28, 33, 35, 43, 47, 98, 100-3
Bean, Mrs 28, 42
Bean Child 98
Black, John 140
Blacksmith's Shop 35, 41, 117-8, 131
Boyle, James 42, 102
Bridge (Waitotorongo Creek) 65
Brind, Capt. W.D. 72, 76
Brown, Rev. Alfred N. 74, 77, 111, 126
Burrows, Mrs 135-6
Busby, James 80
Butler, Rev. John G. 25, 27-8, 31-8, 40-3, 46-7, 50-4, 97-8, 100-4, 106-7, 109, 111, 117-9, 122-4, 126, Appendix 3
Butler, Mrs 27, 33, 43, 46, 52, 97, 101, 105, 108
Butler, Hannah (Anne) 27, 97
Butler, Samuel 27-8, 37-8, 43, 46-7, 51-2, 54, 102, 118-119

Chapel/Church 57, 61, 91, Pt. II Sec. 2
Chapman, Rev. Thomas 76, 78, 81, 111-12, 128-9, 132
Chiefs —
    Apu 44, 46, 54
    Auha 17
    Hauraki 39
    Hengi 72-3

(C cont'd)
    Hihi 109
    Hinaki 35, 41
    Hongi Hika 17-19, 22, 24, 27, 29-30, 33, 38-42, 44-5, 47, 49-51, 53-66, 68, 88, 101-102, 105, 109
    Hongi, Charles 39, 40, 60
    Heke, Hone 89-90, 92, 124, 138
    Kauea 16
    Kawiti 90, 138
    Mahiapoake 17
    Moka 33, 47, 55, 57, 60, 63-4, 89, 110
    Nene, Waka 64
    Muriwai 44
    Pakira 18, 61, 109, 124
    Patuone 80
    Perahiko 31
    Pomare I 72
    Puhi Moana-ariki 16
    Rahiri 16, 17
    Rewa (Manu) 27, 29, 37-41, 47, 49, 53, 55-6, 58, 61-4, 66, 68-9, 80, 89, 103
    Tareha 18, 29, 38, 39, 51, 66, 69, 101, 124
    Te Hotete 17-18
    Te Morenga 22, 31, 39, 42, 47, 57-9, 110
    Te Pahi 21-2
    Te Puhi 21
    Te Tawheta 18
    Tete 44-6, 54
    Tetere 40
    TeNana (Tinana) 29, 110
    Titore Takiri 29, 61, 80
    Toi 40
    Toko-o-te-rangi 16
    'Towee' 51, 52, 109
    Ururoa 61
    Waikato 39, 89
    Wairua 56, 62, 102

(C cont'd)
  Whakaaria 17, 64
  Wharepoaka
  Wharepapa 39
  Wharerahi (Wharenui) 29, 55
Clarke, George 55-7, 59-60, 62-3, 65-8, 73-4, 78, 91, 107, 109-11, 119-20, 122, 124, 127, 129
Clarke, Mrs Martha 63-4, 109-10, 120, 122, 124
Colenso, Wm. 76
Cotton, Rev. Wm. 89, 90-1, 135-6, 148
Cowell, James 52
Cruise, Richard 22
Cunningham, Alan 22, 148

Davis, Charles 57-8
Davis, Rev. Richard 52, 56-60, 74, 92, 109-10, 126-7
Duperrey Expedition 22, 55, 145

Earle, Augustus 23
Edmonds, John 78, 81, 84, 132-3, 140
Edmonds, Samuel 140

Fairburn, Mrs Sarah 28, 35, 42
Fairburn, Richard A. 35
Fairburn, William T. 27-8, 33, 35, 43, 47, 51, 59, 98, 101-3
Firth of Thames 35, 42, 45, 62
Fisher, Rev. Francis 136
Fitzroy, Capt. R. 123-4
Foster, Thomas 42, 101, 103
Franklin, Lady 112, 123, 133

'George' 28
'Gregory' 48
Grey, Governor George 79, 91-2

Hall, Mrs Dinah 100
Hall, Francis 27-8, 32-5, 37-8, 41-7, 50, 55, 101-2, 117-19, 148
Hall, William 28, 97-8, 100-1, 107, 117
Hamlin, Mrs Elizabeth 61-2, 72
Hamlin, Rev. James 61-2, 64, 66-7, 72, 74, 91, 122, 127, 145-6
Hansen, Thomas 24, 47
Hawaiiki 15
Hobbs, Rev. John 129
Hobson, Capt. W. 88
Hokianga 32, 42, 44, 50, 59-60, 62-3, 67, 128-9
Hongi's European House 54, 56, 63, 65, 68-9

'Jane' 52, 105-6
Jowett, William 29-30

Kahikatearoa 38, 57, 100-1, 103, 148
Kaikohe 90
Kaipara 16, 35, 55, 60, 62
Kaitaia 50, 81, 131
Kawakawa 28, 59, 101, 118
Kemp, Mrs Charlotte 27, 37, 43, 46, 52, 84, 91, 108, 113, 124
Kemp, Charlotte 139
Kemp, Elizabeth 88
Kemp, Ethel 140
Kemp, Frank 140
Kemp, Henry Tacy 37, 85
Kemp, James (Jnr.) 133, 140, 150
Kemp, James (Snr.) 11, 25, 27, 31-5, 38, 40-6, 50, 53-4, 56, 59, 65, 67, 76, 84-5, 87-8, 91-2, 101, 103, 106, 110, 112-3, 118-121, 124, 127-9, 132-4, 138
Kemp, Richard 138-9
Kemp's House (1st) 25, 35, 52, 59, 68, 78, 97, 98, 104, 105, 112, 132, 139
Kemp House (2nd) (Mission House) 10-12, 25, 34, 52, 54, 59, 62, 67, 78, 81, 91, Pt II Sec. 1, 119, 131, 136
Kempthorne, Sampson 135
Kendall, Susannah 42
Kendall, Rev. Thomas 10-11, 24, 28, 33, 39-42, 47, 49-54, 59, 109, 119, 138
Kendall, Thomas S. 103
Kent, Capt. 69
Kerikeri Basin 11, 22, 24, 56, 92, 101, 117, 122, 131, 146
Kerikeri Inlet 12, 22, 28, 31, 42, 45, 63, 91, 122, 126, 128, 131-2
Kerikeri River 24, 35, 38, 55-6, 62, 68, 100, 109, 111, 131, 145-7
King, John 24, 28, 74, 107
Kinghorne —, 129, 131, 146
Kororareka (Russell) 37, 50-1, 66, 72, 74
Kororipo 10, 17, 24, 46, 49, 54, 62, 68, 75, 87, 89, 92, 94, 102, 104, 124
'Koshaddei' 44

Lee, John 37, 38, 42, 102
Leith, William 22
Leigh, Rev. Samuel 24, 36, 52, 68, 106
Leigh, Mrs Catherine 52, 106
Lewington, W. 129

McCrae, Ensign 29-30
Manawaora Bay 42

Index

(M cont'd)
Mangonui (Te Puna) Inlet 18, 38, 51-2, 85
Markham, Edward 149
Marsden, Rev. Samuel 21-2, 24-7, 30-7, 40, 42-3, 45-7, 51-4, 60-1, 64, 73-5, 78, 92, 98, 110, 118-9, 126-8, 131, 145, 149
Matauwhi Bay 50
Mathew, Felton 112
Matthews, Rev. Joseph 50, 81
Maunsell, Rev. Robert 139
Mission House (Kemp House) 10-12, 25, 34, 52, 54, 59, 62, 67, 78, 81, 91, Pt. II Sec 1, 119, 131, 136
Mokoia (Panmure, Auckland) 35-6, 41, 44, 51
Moremonui, Battle of 58
Morgan, Rev. John 81
Motuihe Island (Waitemata Harbour) 35-6, 41
Moturoa Island 21

Nicholas, John L. 22, 24, 145
New South Wales 36-7, 42, 46, 59-61, 74-6, 98, 100, 106, 119, 126-8, 131
New Zealand Company (1st) 63, 111
New Zealand Company (2nd) 87
New Zealand Historic Places Trust 12-13, 113, 141
Nisbet, Alfred (Ben) 111-2, 131-2, 134
Norris, Ebenezer 139

Ohaeawai 91, 138
Okura 31, 36-9, 46-7, 51
Okuratope Pa 17, 62
Omapere, Lake 22, 57, 73
Oruru (Doubtless Bay) 62

Paihia 10, 51, 59, 61-4, 66, 74, 76, 78, 80-1, 84, 110-12, 119, 122, 126-8, 132
Papakauri 146
Parengaroa 23, 52, 57, 61, 109
Paroa Bay 37, 62, 66, 68
Parrott, William 128-9, 131-3
Pawero 131
Printing 75-6
Puckey, Elizabeth 27-8
Puckey, William G. (Jnr.) 27-8, 50, 62, 81, 120
Puckey, William (Snr.) 27-8, 35, 41, 47, 49-50, 54, 56, 58, 62, 102, 109
Puckey, Mrs Matilda 27-8, 62
Pukenui (Te Ahuahu) 57, 59, 72
Puketi 149
Puketotara River 68, 147-8
Puketutu 91
Puriri (Thames) 81

Rangihoua 10, 19, 24, 26, 28-9, 32-3, 37-8, 42, 45-7, 72, 74-5, 77, 101-2, 104, 107, 110, 117, 119, 122, 126

(R cont'd)
Ross, Sir James Clark 149
Russell, Richard 28

St. John's College 89, 91, 124, 135, 138
Selwyn, Bishop George Augustus 89, 91, 124, 133-6, 138, 150
Selwyn, Mrs Sarah 89, 134-6
Shepherd, Mrs Harriet 37, 43, 57-8, 72, 84
Shepherd, James 31, 35-8, 43-4, 46, 50-2, 54, 56-8, 61, 74, 81, 84-5, 104, 109, 110, 118-9, 126, 132-3
Ships — *Active* 37, 129, 131-2
  Boyd 21
  Brampton 52-3, 119
  Coquille 55
  Coromandel 35
  Dromedary 30, 37, 40, 55, 98
  Hazard H.M.S. 91
  Herald 56, 61-2, 66, 68, 127
  Karere 85, 128-9, 132
  Macquarie 60
  North Star H.M.S. 91
  Seringapatum 37
  Tory 88
  Vansittart 47
Skudders Beach 23
Spickman, William 52, 54, 61, 132
Smith, James 75-6
Stack, Rev. James 63
Stone Store 10-12, 78, 80, 85, 91, 101, 112, Sec. II Pt. 3, 146
Stutchbury, Samuel 22, 145
Styles and Harris (Hokianga) 128-9

Taiamai 22, 58, 126
Tahuna 73
Taua, Mary 85, 124
Taylor, Rev. Richard 23
Te Kohanga (Waikato R.) 139
Te Puna 16, 18, 21, 74-5, 78 , 81, 84, 126
Te Tii 38, 52-4
Toharanui 85, 118
Treaty of Waitangi 11, 88
Tribes —
  Aupouri 16
  Hokianga/Ngapuhi 16, 39, 59, 72, 80, 148
  Kaipara Tribes 47, 58-9
  Ngaere Raumati 18, 40
  Ngai Tawake 58, 66, 73-4, 79
  Ngapuhi 15-18
  Ngati Awa 16-17
  Ngati Maru 41-2, 44

(T cont'd)
   Ngati Miru (hapu) 16-18
   Ngati Paoa 35, 42
   Ngati Pou 63
   Ngatirehia (sub-tribe) 18, 38, 124, 148
   Rarawa 16
   Waikato Tribes 47-8, 56
Tungaroa 47, 52
Turner Rev. Nathaniel 25
Turner, Mrs Ann 68

Wade, William 85
Waianiwaniwa Falls (Rainbow Falls) 12, 100-1, Pt. II Sec. 4
Waiapu, James 85
Waikare River 28, 98, 101-2, 104
Waikato District 16, 62, 139
Waimate 17-18, 29, 31-2, 38, 44, 52-3, 55, 57-60, 62-4, 66, 68, 72, 74, 75, 76, 78, 80, 84, 89-91, 111, 123-4, 126-8, 131, 133, 136, 138-9
Waipapa 16, 38, 51, 72, 126, 149
Wairoa Stream 17, 24, 29, 44, 46-8, 56, 87, 89, 131
Waitangi 62, 72
Waitemata Harbour 35-6, 98
Waitotorongo Creek 28, 65, 67, 75, 102, 117, 119
Waiuku 139
'Wattoo' 120
Wesleyans (Methodists) 51, 118, 129
Whangarei 51, 68, 91, 149
Whangaroa 16-17, 21, 33, 42, 51-2, 59-60, 62-4, 84-5, 91, 118, 132
Wharepoke Falls (Kerikeri Falls) 12, Pt. II Sec. 4
Wood, Peleg 133, 136
Williams, Rev. Henry 22, 51-2, 54, 59, 60-2, 67, 69, 74-5, 78, 80-1, 85, 104, 109, 111, 112, 126, 128-9, 131, 133
Williams, Mrs Jane (William) 10, 61, 64
Williams, Mrs Marianne (Henry) 10, 24, 52, 64, 104-6, 108, 122, 146
Williams, Rev. William 10, 61-2, 69, 74-5, 77, 111-2, 126

Yate, Rev. William 10-12, 66-9, 72-80, 111-2, 121, 123, 126-8, 145-6